WHAT WISE MEN DO

THE SECRET WORLD OF CONAN DOYLE, BRAM STOKER, JULES VERNE AND THE UNSEEN HAND

PHILIP GARDINER

First published 21st February 2009
by

The Temple Publications
PO Box 47
Watchet
Somerset
TA23 0WT
United Kingdom

ISBN 978-0-9555970-9-1

Cover design by Lee Yarlett
Printed in the UK by
CPI William Clowes Beccles NR34 7TL

Contents

Foreword v

Introduction x

Chapter 1: Paracelsus – The Sign of the White Horse 1

Chapter 2: Religion and Alchemists 13

Chapter 3: H. G. Wells – The Man on the Moon 34

Chapter 4: Jules Verne and the Power of Imagination 48

Chapter 5: Bram Stoker – Beware of Invasion 72

Chapter 6: Bob Kane and the World of the Bats 92

Chapter 7: Sir Arthur Conan Doyle – Even the Wise Get Confused 102

Chapter 8: Magic, Mind, God 120

Chapter 9: A Message from the Past 138

Bibliography 143

Index 149

Other titles 152

Foreword

The title of this book may at first appear to be slightly sexist, *What Wise Men Do*, as opposed to what wise "people" do. Anybody who knows me will understand that I am not sexist at all and that I would have good reason for choosing such a title. That reason is simple, quite apart from the "men" simply meaning humans in this respect, the majority of the people we shall be discussing in this book are men and lived in a time that was very much a man's world. Women did not have the vote, and if they did, then they were very often guided by their husbands. These same husbands held the purse strings, were the main workers, the business leaders, the politicians and the priests. Women, in general, were regarded as almost second-class citizens. Thankfully things have changed, albeit not totally to the satisfaction of all, but we can thank those women of history who stood their ground for the feminine cause.

So this book is sexist in respect of the fact I have chosen men from periods when women had little hope of rising through any kind of ranks. There were many women who were highly influential and did create literary works that hold great interest. The mystic, Madame Blavatsky, was one such influential character and we shall in fact be discussing her later in the book. Blavatsky stands out as a strong-willed character who certainly caused changes in society and using knowledge from within secret traditions. And this is steering me closer to the point of this book. It may be that men have predominately written upon the esoteric, the occult, the hidden world, because the world of the secret society has traditionally been a male dominated arena. Freemasonry has for centuries been dominated by males and, even today, female membership is only accepted into specific Lodges and then governed by men. The same is true of many such organizations and some of them, such as the Church are not so secret.

The well-spring of ideas, knowledge, concepts and ultimately, wisdom, that emerges from being introduced and involved in the rituals and symbolism of ancient occult practices can often be overbearing for the creatively minded. Many individuals wish to express their new-found knowledge and yet are often restricted by the very membership of the organization to which they are attached and from where they have derived their knowledge. "It is not for the profound" as one Freemason once told me. However, the creative mind can often discover ways and means of overcoming these restrictions and not least of these is the world of fiction.

There are many examples that can be used to express this as fact and that is the point of this work – that men who were either members of secretive organizations or were in the know, actually did find a way of producing works of great creativity which did express their knowledge. From the stories of King Arthur and the Holy Grail to the modern film series of *The Matrix*, esoteric and psychological concepts are discussed and portrayed in fiction and many scholars believe that this can often explain the longevity and success of such tales. The tales of the Grail dealt with the spiritual, political and psychological aspects of living in a specific time and *The Matrix* does precisely the same for today. The Middle Ages were a dark time for many people, with warfare, disease and social unrest rife. The only methods known for dealing with these issues and many more, was the Church and its concept of the next life. The only way of escaping the often terrible existence, full of sin and death, was to do the bidding of the spiritual masters, toe the line and achieve salvation – to be saved from this torment of hell. However, there had been an underground and ancient method of self-enlightenment now, whilst alive and which had been sent underground by a jealous Church. Such legendary groups as the Gnostics and the Templars speak to us of this hidden message. This message was one of self-discovery and growth in this life, not necessarily awaiting the saviour in the next. The over-arching element here is the strength of those in power. It was the Church which maintained almost Empirical control over the masses whilst their petty Kings and Queens squabbled over land. The Church collected taxes, land and the worship of the people and allowed the Kings and Queens to rule, by the authority of the Church's God. Undermining this massive power-base was not tolerated and so "heretics" such as the Cathars, who preached self-illumination and the divinity within (esoteric) as opposed to without (exoteric), were stamped out by the bully-boys of the Church.

Today, many people would be surprised to discover that very little has in fact changed. There are still great powers in the world who need to control the mind and soul of the people and use the world of the media to do so. In times past the media was the Preacher, the stained glass windows and the few repetitive words sung hypnotically as hymns. Today it is the television, the internet, printed matter, mobile phones and radio. We are told that life can be good for us now, if only we buy product 'x'. In order to do so, we must work hard and toe the line – thus beginning a cycle that later in life the debt-ridden individual, even if enlightened, finds difficult to escape from. The question arises in the minds of those who have become aware of this massive amorphous scam; "What do I do?" Am I happy to remain part of this system, or should I opt out into a world I know to be true, but which may be fraught with danger because of those who control the system? This is the world of *The Matrix* and although that film is portrayed as fiction and many people simply see it as such, there are in fact incredible truths spoken of within it. The selection of the correct pill, red or blue, that Neo (new man) must decide upon is the choice we must all take. Let me use a few examples:

My son came home recently from school and was talking about how a large group of Gypsies had taken over a piece of common land (land owned in common by the people). He explained how the other children had mocked them and even thrown cans at their mobile homes. All the usual "isms" erupted from this small segment of society, revealing that the children were being "well-trained" for their future life on the hamster's wheel and as self-perpetuating guardians of the "correct order of society". The Gypsies were thieves, homosexual or perverted, not "English", dirty and a drain on society. The intense prejudice would be quite startling if it were not for the fact that it is unfortunately not a rarity.

I pointed out, in balance, the actual facts as we know them. These are humans just like you and I and have children, husbands and wives, friends, loves, concerns and indeed hates and prejudices. There is no evidence to suggest that the straight, white male who knifed a young girl in the city the previous night was a Gypsy. In fact he had a job, a mortgaged house, a new car and was a fully paid up member of society. What he did do was suffer from boredom standing in a fast food restaurant all day. His answer was to drink profusely, unable to deal with his own inner angst, because nobody had ever taught him anything different than to buy goods and grow a field of debt, get a job and settle down. Nobody had ever mentioned philosophy to this child or told him that he was part of a wonderful intricate system far higher and much more profound than humanity's - nature.

The evidence does not, in fact, reveal that Gypsies, nor any other kind of group to which we hurl prejudiced hatred, are any more prone to the deadly sins than individuals extracted from our own so-called wonderful society. Society is society - it is a reflection of the inner turmoil of the human mind and until we deal with this chaotic consciousness, we shall never have a decent society upon which to build. Ancient psychological concepts of balance and nature have been fostered within the heart of some organizations and there have been men who have wished for this to nurture a new world. But the greed and chaos of the human mind seems to always overcome and eventually the rot sets in. The in-built and perfectly natural urge of prejudice is a function of protection and defence and understanding this helps the individual balance out his or her judgements. However, those in positions of power often have no intention of subduing prejudice because it can work for their own desired ends. One only has to look at Nazi Germany to understand that.

Unless fathers and mothers take the time to teach their children about such things then the cycle will continue forever and society as a whole will gradually lose all sight of balanced thought. As H. G. Wells once said, we teach our children about the philosopher, about when and where he lived, but we neglect to teach them about the philosophy. What is more important? Does it really matter when Socrates lived, or is it more important to stretch the mind of the young into processes of thought that will generate creative thinking for a better society? Our present method is almost as bad as teaching the medical student about when and where a medicine was discovered and neglecting to tell them how to administer it, let alone what it was for in the first place.

The Gypsies that my son saw were no better or worse than any other human, they just lived a different lifestyle. The police came within minutes of their arrival and they were moved on, because society could not accept them in their presence. And we watch the skies hoping to spot an alien craft? I know I wouldn't land.

The knowledge and wisdom of firstly discovering the self and throwing off the cloaks of deceit we have taken on and then moving forward and understanding that no matter what we do in life, unless it makes you a good, balanced person then it is of little worth has been around for a long time. But society throws up many distractions for the masses and so it remains hidden. Films like *The Matrix* sent out a message to those who wondered and saw glitches in the world around them. But it is not about creating yet another new religion or building a religious home in Zion for man to stare in awe at. Zion is within each of us and we build it ourselves. Only then will society manifest the true nature and light of wisdom as a collective whole directly from the source of the energy of nature. Let me explain:

The universe is a charged energy system working on a set of ratios that have been discovered by mathematicians and scientists (and were hinted at by several ancient philosophers who intuitively knew). It is not "the" universe, as if it were separate from ourselves, instead it is our womb, our kindergarten, our home. We came from it, into it and cannot be parted, no matter how much reductionism we apply. We are therefore walking, talking, mostly conscious elements of the universe itself. Think about that for a second. You are a conscious part of the universe, you express the mathematical ratios of "creation" itself. Within you wells up the energy of evolution. This is not some New Age philosophy, nor is it religion, it is instead perfectly scientific fact, but it is also profound because we are aware of it. Because man has become aware of his own self within this remarkable thing we call the universe he has also become aware of his own fatality. This secondary issue to consciousness has caused the imaginations of man to run riot with speculation and hope for an answer to the loss of self at death. The creations from within the mind of man have then been used as tools against man by other men. If we can find rest in the knowledge of who we are and what we are part of, remembering that so far everything else seems to be conjecture, then we will remain relatively free. Accepting the fiction of others such as Heaven and Hell, will simply lead us up the garden path into the trap of control. As Conan Doyle discovered and as we shall see, accepting "not knowing" does not come easily to anybody; even those with great minds such as Doyle.

So, what do wise men do when they live in a system that is controlling, in a time that is prejudiced and they discover wisdom many years after stepping onto the hamster's wheel? They try to help those that will follow them and hope that somebody somewhere in the future of mankind will begin to teach the children about the philosophies they leave, and not about the man who wrote them nor where they lived.

Introduction

What is it that we are searching for as humans? Are we looking for happiness, fulfilment, an easy life? Or are we searching for something more, something profound? The truth is that many of us do not even consider such things, instead we simply live out our lives looking for the next thing, a better existence, a fresh income, a way of appearing more powerful or impressive to those around us. Do we really consider the affects we have on society, our friends, our loved ones? Maybe we do, maybe we don't. Each person will be different and have a different view.

And yet, across time there have been many who have sought out deeper meaning to their lives and to existence itself. No matter how far back we delve into the past of human history we will discover a yearning to know more. Whether we discover ancient man erecting large monoliths to measure by the stars and worship their immense power over time or whether we uncover the lost teachings of priests from a forgotten age, what we find will always have a resonance with us today. For we are the same human, with the same beginning and end, trapped in a wheel or life and death, grasping for understanding of who and what we are.

Over the course of thousands of years our ancestors have left us great wisdom traditions in literature, ritual and symbolism. And over those millennia man has always sought out that wisdom from his ancestors. Was it not Plato who told us the tale of Atlantis and how the Athenians looked backwards to a greater and more wise time? And before them it was the Egyptians! And today we still seek out that same wisdom.

In each age the thinking man has sought out answers to the greatest questions of existence and in each age he has had to come to the same conclusions as the last – that ultimately we cannot prove anymore than that which we see and even that is debatable. He is often left only with faith.

This book delves into the mind of men who spent their lives seeking greater wisdom and knowledge and (possibly like you) I too am a journeyman on the road to wherever it may lead. I do not claim to be wise, for the man who does so has much to learn, but I am seeking and every day I learn more about myself and existence. I believe that the individuals we shall be examining in this book were extraordinary. They had focus, desire and intuition, but did they discover their truth? I leave that to the reader to decide.

For me, when I see a leaf on a tree I see an extension of the very energy that sprang from the Big Bang itself (wherever that came from?) The tree begins with a single seed; it grows tall searching for the light and absorbing water, branching off and bringing new life, new leaves and seeds. I see this wonderful pattern in everything with variations I need not expand upon here. I also see this in ourselves. We are born from the seed, we grow, plant more seeds, seek the light and absorb the waters of wisdom. And yet we have become conscious entities, thoughtful descendants of the energy of the Big Bang itself. This thought, to me, is profound and is why I decided to write, produce and direct a film recently called *Ancient Code* (see www.ancientcode.com). This was my attempt to produce a work like Jules Verne or H. G. Wells that utilised the media of the day to get a message across. It is not my message, it is "the" message discovered and filtered by the men in this book and more over thousands of years. The following is a transcript of the film and I humbly submit it as a work in progress with more yet to come.

Ancient Code

The Western world has found itself to be a mass of individuals with little comprehension that their own interaction with each other and existence itself actually has cause and affect.

Individualisation is indeed part of the problem in the West

In the Orient, especially in India, we often find a very different reality. Here we find that dark and light are not separate entities but actually co-existent realities, just as their myriad of gods are not separate entities, but actually manifestations of the Oneness of all things. They simply have different faces and forms as mankind is a reflection of Nature itself.

In the East man is part of Nature, not subject to it or master of it. As a consequence he is part of the collective, universal soul, a walking, talking part of conscious Nature.

Much of the blame for the West's disassociation from Nature can be given to its modern form of Christianity and current version of science. To those in certain schools of esoteric thought, highly influenced by Eastern concepts, science was a method of understanding Nature better for the good of the whole, the One. It was a way simply of becoming conscious of and with Nature.

Today, we have more often than not, reduced science to a means of classifying and empirically justifying what we can prove or not prove to be "true" based on perspectives and calculations from a highly limited viewpoint.

Christianity itself was reduced from its original Gnostic, Eastern concepts to an Empirical law making power to capitalise on and control others. Divide and conquer was the mantra and so mankind's own mind was divided not just from one another's, but from the very concept of his Oneness with Nature itself.

This division has left behind a stark emptiness that simply cannot be filled with the materialism our modern society has replaced it with. The many faces of God – Nature itself – cannot be replaced with the endless stream of Hollywood deities, no matter how hard we try.

The world is at a point of crisis, people feel an impending doom, that time itself is moving too fast, rushing us headlong into bad choices and fewer and fewer alternatives.

On one hand we embrace the materialism and power games of the darker nature and accept that this will entail yet more denial of our true will, our true beings. On the other we yearn to lose that fabricated self we have become accustomed to in-order to discover a more real self, one that is one directly connected to Nature.

The self we perceive as our own is in truth a self built up from layers of propaganda and mind control, from indoctrination and rules and laws made by others in order to create a "civilised and orderly society"

This unseen force, has evolved into a massive and unwieldy machine, which traverses the world gaining more ground every day. It is unstoppable only because we allow it to be so, to propagate within our minds and effect our daily lives.

The Ancient Code is simple, it is so simple that it cannot be easily understood by the minds of those confused with the chatter of technology, materialism and the false doctrines of controlling religions and organisations. There is only one way to fully realise and access the ancient code and that is to free the mind, completely, of all things that lie above our inherent survival and natural being. To free our minds of the noise of the outside world that is suppressing our higher selves.

Eternal truths were past down from ancient times via the Gnostics, Sufi's and other caretakers of Ancient Wisdom. These found a home in India and enveloped the East; they lived for millennia in Egypt; they survived Christianity's onslaught under the cloak of Alchemy and today it is time for mankind to rediscover these truths and reclaim the natural balance of body mind and spirit.

Only by freeing the mind can the whole realisation come through that we are part of Nature, not separate from it. Only by understanding science via this intuition can we truly do science. If we over complicate Nature with our words and devices then we lose the path. Many so-called mathematical explanations for how Nature works are said to be "sick equations" because they appear too complicated. Nature is not so complex - instead it is ratio built upon ratio empowered by energy interacting in the same way on every level, whether particle or planetary sphere.

So what is this Nature?

Hermann Hesse, the Nobel prize-winning writer said, *"It is wrong to think that Nature is the enemy of man, something to be conquered. Rather, we should look upon Nature as a mother, and should peaceably surrender ourselves to it. If we take that attitude, we will simply feel that we are returning to the Universe as all other things do, all animals and all plants. We are all just infinitesimal parts of the Whole. It is absurd to rebel; we must deliver ourselves to the great current."* (*My Belief: Essays in the Life and Art*, Hermann Hesse, edited an with an introduction by Theodore Ziolkowski, translated by Denver Lindley, New York: Farrar, Straus and Giroux, 1974.)

This current that Hesse Speaks of is key to understanding our part in the Whole. We are beings of energy, empowered by energy brought into life from the spark of procreation - the physical union of opposites

Even greater psychological empowerment comes from same spark and pattern of nature mirrored in the mind. It is the Gnostic and Eastern concept of uniting the dark and light, the left and right, within our very minds. Not "being" divided, but being Whole within ourselves and truly and emotionally connecting thereafter to the Wholeness of Nature itself, because we will have achieved what Nature itself perpetually seeks for – balance and union._

Its is clear that the dominating Western powers have promulgated a divisive concept of the "persona" or individualisation, causing a sickness in our society and the way we see our world and our existence. We view all things as separate and thus we classify them as such with one another and therefore the problem continues to expand and multiply more and more rapidly. Society, science, philosophy and everything else becomes competitive instead of united. With the added incentive of the emotive creation of religion and belief systems, from whatever angle, we distance ourselves from each other even further.

And yet, Nature has remained the same. Our 'Nature' is still inside us. Still lurking beneath these human creations awaiting discovery like a lost treasure. This is the true quest for the Holy Grail. This is the real code we need to break. It is the code of our very own mindsets and we are the key.

Each of us must come to this truth in their own way. For the vast majority these truths will not reveal themselves through words, which are often masks for lies, unless those words depict a symbolic journey or quest.

For some, ratio and mathematics has revealed great esoteric secrets; for others it is music, emotion, experience, chance meetings and observation, perhaps even a synchronicity. In all respects these are early forms of symbols. Our ancestors observed the world of Nature, both the external physical Nature and the internal Nature of man. They did not write down words to express their understanding. Instead they interpreted via symbolic language, creating musical forms which mirrored the observable frequencies and wave-forms in Nature and images that had multi-layered meanings such as those of Egypt.

By observing what has been placed for us upon the landscape, in great Temples, in ancient monuments, in music, even underlying meanings hidden in fables, we can begin to unlock the code and thereby begin to free our own mind of the constraints of modern living.

The Temple is a place that symbolised the Universe, both physically and spiritually. It was a place where all things were unified, a place where we were meant to gain understanding and reminded of this principle, that we are all and all is in us.

That in the moment we enter a symbolic place, we were to remember this fact. This is why Temples, Churches and places of so-called worship, include symbols of Nature, of the great cycles of time and of our place in it.

The story of the Holy Grail is one of the greatest of symbolic tales. It has been re-interpreted thousands of times mostly with modern eyes.

The Grail stories we have heard, originated hundreds of years ago, we have a murky concept that they originated in some dark pagan, even medieval past . There is however, evidence that they derived originally from Gnostic concepts with links into Indian and Egyptian myths.

Whatever the truth, it appears that they speak of Nature and reunification. The Grail is the symbol of the ultimate goal. It contains the energy or blood of the one who was in-tune with the Divine, which was Nature, the essence of life as we know it for God is within us all as both the Christians, Muslims and other religions believe.

We must all seek the Grail, for this is the ultimate quest, but we must ask the right questions of it, to prove that our mind has been perfected and purified of unnatural desires, that we are ready to receive an answer and that we will be responsible with the knowledge if given a glimpse of it. But we must not ask questions of it that reflect our world of materialism, but instead seek to simply connect with "it" for what it is.

Herein lies a great truth to connecting with the Atman or the centre of all, a thing that has no beginning and no end, something powerful beyond our wildest imaginations, something that just is…The great sphinx of Egypt stares out at the world and the stars above it eternally, pristinely gazing into infinity…into the abyss… its message is there for all who seek it, yet so many cannot abandon the false self's they have in fact helped to create, to peel back the layers of conditioning to see the simple truth perpetually offered by this ancient monument.

In our material world, our eyes and thoughts are too often drawn toward the gold and jewels of the chalice, yet we cannot see what resides within, Whom does it serve? one might ask… Its serves the one who serves it…

This energy, or blood of the grail, is within us all, whether man or woman, big or small. The problem has always been that we are simply not aware of it. Even when the infamous

Gospel of Thomas was written this was true and in the words of the one they identified as the Christ we can see this truth:

> *"If you bring forth what is within you, what you bring forth will save you. If you do not bring forth what is within you, what you do not bring forth will destroy you."*

Nature can save you and Nature can kill you, physically and psychologically.

Our question today has to be, are we willing to be saved by ourselves? Or are we perfectly happy to absolve ourselves of responsibility and meander along blaming others for our woes and misfortunes, for the things we seemingly cannot bring ourselves to achieve?

These are the words of a true saviour, words that come from and speak to our inner being, which knows that these words speak of spiritual or psychological fulfilment and not always physical and financial safety. The wind will indeed blow us in every direction but how will we set our sail?

These truths will not necessarily enable you to get rich quick, or empower you to be the greatest leader of men for power hungry leaders. This is not a "secret" or "quantum" method of bettering your fellow man. These are truths, plain and simple. Nature is Nature, it breeds, it nurtures, it grows, it kills and dies. It is dark and light, as too are we. If you ask for great materials riches of the Grail you will most likely be ignored. If you are purified and fortunate enough to be given the message of the grail you will however, have riches beyond your wildest dreams.

But what stops us seeing these truths? The same thing that enables us to be aware of them - consciousness. A Pueblo Indian once told Carl Jung, that white men thought with their heads. When Jung asked him how he thought, the Indian responded that he naturally thought with his heart. Jung himself said that "white man" in reality tended only to think with their tongues.

This is a truth that we must confront, that it is the individual consciousness, which stops the unconscious, and therefore Natural self, to be revealed. We do have to act consciously to see the hidden world of truth, but the ultimate paradox is that we have to deny the conscious self, which has become loaded with materialism and over saturated with endless streams of modern day stimulus. We have to cast off the old self and be born anew to what we really are – Natural beings in a Natural Universe, mirroring the beauty and ratio of its energy and frequency in so many ways. Understanding or being enlightened to this energy enables us to interact better with the energy of everything else around us. We must think with our hearts, our very centre, the intuitive self.

A simple example is how we interact with our pets, our dogs, our cats, let alone one another. If we pull and push, instead of working together in a calm and steady way, we will in most cases will not achieve the symbiotic union or relationship that we truly seek. A dog who wishes to be with his pack leader and respects him will walk along in harmony._

The same is true in all levels of our lives, including the way we interact with each other. We must understand the very simple energy of Nature in-order to deal with the situations that arise… this requires intuition, which is not ultimately a conscious act.

So how to begin? How do we release ourselves of the world that does not make us truly happy within?

The first question has to be…. are you ready?

Unless man is willing to accept that the way in which he has organised his mind and his society is flawed then we have no starting point. Ask yourself, am I truly happy? Do I improve my family and friends with my thought's words and deeds? Do I contribute to my Society? Am I missing something altogether?

Should I believe all that I am told by those who we assume to be qualified to lead?

If you have asked these questions….in truth and honesty…. and you wish to proceed to unlock the inner self and discover Nature then you are on the Grail quest.

You must begin by destroying your gods.

All through life we have been told that those with the most money and power are superior to us and to our shame we have accepted these pretences. We have been told that icons of religions held literal truths, that walking on water was a literally miracle…and so we had to bend our minds to an unnatural thing. This has taken us from the path of Nature, the underlying current of all that is, to fixate on things that we are told occurred that are wholly unnatural.

The West has believed the *Da Vinci Code* fiction that Christ married Mary Magdalene, simply because it fails to see the symbolic language of these concepts – that the opposites must unite and balance be brought for the true energy or blood to continue in it's beautiful cycle. This is indeed great symbolism, mirroring Nature itself in symbolic fable and we have missed the point entirely because we are no longer in-tune with it.

Everything must be questioned and every god of Hollywood must be in their proportional place within your mind. All men are men and all women, women, nothing more, nothing less, no matter the title bestowed by man. Whether we call them Highness, Pope or Celebrity, these titles are human errors of judgement. A man who calls himself wise has much to learn.

We must seek our true self. Carl Jung said that the self is a circle whose centre is everywhere and whose circumference is nowhere.

Seek the King within you not without. Do not look to others to fulfil your natural desires or absolve yourself of all and any responsibility. Accept your responsibility and with the energy of the force of Nature within you rise above the dark desires of greed, envy and hate towards the light. Mirror nature, we wake in the light and we have no part in the dark.

Once we have absolved our minds with regard to our desire for gods and misleading messiahs, we will be free of the desire to emulate them and so… we can turn to higher and higher things. To pursue our own evolution to become the things we imagine and to achieve them in the physical world. The time is now to go outside and observe Nature in order to understand the inner nature of all living things. You will see that Nature itself, whether tree, a cat or dog, does not live its life according to what happened yesterday or what may happen tomorrow, but simply lives now.

If we constantly worry and obsess on what happened before, then we are literally leading and instructing our imaginations to take over in our minds and feed us an endless list of negative assumptions about our futures.

Understanding this part of our Nature enables us to recognise that these are false dialogues inside the mind, however useful they may be in certain circumstances.. such as predicting a tree will fall when it tilts heavily in a strong wind.

These thoughts need to be balanced and kept in check, we do not need to emulate Nature and live in the now, we need to *release and embrace* our Nature and live in the now.

We need to free ourselves of what has already happened and not create a lesser future for ourselves by imagining it so. Our future is important and measures must be taken to provide security for oneself and ones family but not at the expense of living in fear of it.

If we live now, according to the beautiful ratios, rhythms and patterns of Nature with awareness, respect and strength and a will that is true to ourselves then we shall create a beautiful future for ourselves and others.

The wind will blow, how will we set your sail?

The true power of understanding Nature for us is no different to that seen by our ancestors. It was magical to be able to read a pack or herd, to predict the seasons, to know exactly what to say or do for a loved one at the right time.

But more than that – it was ultimately fulfilling. Such connection to Nature that only openness can bring, releases an energy so profound that there is no method of expressing it with words. This sense of unification enlightens the soul, it brightens the day and makes the night a sound sleep, it gladdens the heart for it reaches to the very centre of ourselves, it reconnects Nature with Nature and we become conscious of it and in awe of its power.

Nature holds the secret to the greatest of powers, and we must wield it with love.

Today our science is coming full circle and revealing to us that we are part of the Whole. For well over a hundred years science has reduced all that we have observed into names and categories and experimented with them as if they themselves were Gods. Men did not try to live with our world, they tried to use it for our own ends, by ignorant ambition seeking to tame it....to control it....to no true avail..

Now that our knowledge is finally beginning to reveal the ancient code yet again, will we listen and learn?

The film, *Ancient Code*, has much more, for I spent many weeks collecting the thoughts of individuals and merging them with the above narration. These individuals are very much like the men included in this book. Some were Freemasons, others seekers, and others men who have gained their own special immortality from their TV presence. But in each case, whatever the background, they all agreed on one thing – we are all connected, we are all part of Nature and separation from that understanding, that wisdom and knowledge, has divided us not just from Nature but from our very selves.

Chapter 1

Paracelsus – The Sign of the White Horse

There are few men who have caused such extremes of outspoken support and hatred as Paracelsus. His life is one that revealed the duality of mankind. It highlighted the old and the new, the unimaginative and the dreamers. He was a man born on the rift of change as Mother Church underwent her reformation. Martin Luther opened the eyes of society to the words of the Bible and the jealous Latin of the hierarchy gave way to common tongue. And this was an example of the way the rest of society was thinking – why should we hold back progress for the sake of the clerics? Even the Pope was receiving bad press for his Pagan orgies and so the people needed new guidance. Explorers were scouring the globe and discovering new lands, people, riches, foods, medicines and influences. This was an exciting time for many, the birth pangs of a new era, but the old mother would have killed her new child had she been allowed.

Paracelsus was a man at the cutting edge of this new period. He had energy, wit and wisdom, but he was still vulnerable to the power of those stuck in a rut.

Born on the 11th November 1493 in Einsiedeln, Switzerland, Theophrastus Philippus Aureolus Bombastus von Hohenheim later gave himself the name Paracelsus, meaning 'beside/better than or similar to Celsus', the Roman physician of the 1st century AD. His father was a chemist and as a youth he worked as an analyst at a nearby mine where he discovered the wonder and science of geology, rocks and minerals. At the

The infamous Paracelsus pictured without facial hair. A coincidence?

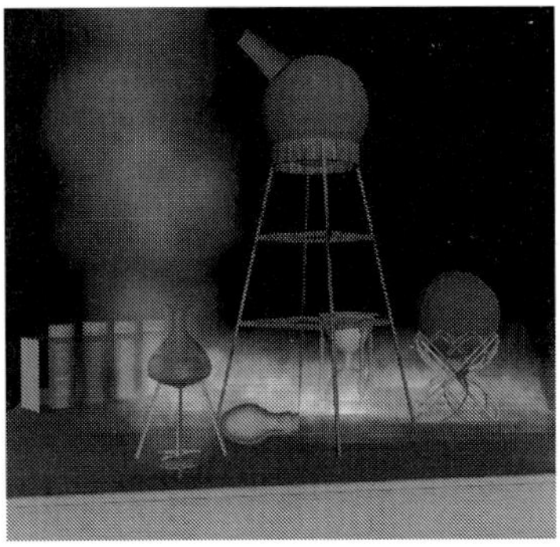

The standard vision of alchemy as some kind of chemists workshop.

tender age of sixteen he began studying medicine at Basel University and then later on at Vienna, gaining a doctorate from the University of Ferrara. At the time chemistry and alchemy were little different and in fact were seen to be both the search for ultimate truth and the science of nature. In the search for these truths Paracelsus traveled extensively, visiting Egypt, Arabia, the Holy Land and Constantinople. He brought back to Europe a wealth of knowledge, including medical treatments from the enlightened medieval Islamic world, which would bring him fame. On the face of it Paracelsus rejected Gnostic traditions, instead leaning towards Hermetic, Pythagorean and neoplatonic philosophies. However many scholars believe that his supposed rejection of Gnostic philosophies were not in fact substantiated due to his Aristotelian Hermetical reasonings. In fact the truth of the matter is simple. It was the magical elements of Agrippa and Flamel that Paracelsus was not in agreement with - seeing them as unreal, even though he was a practising astrologer. There is, in fact, a little contradiction in this reasoning, for Paracelsus devoted several chapters in his book *Archidoxes of Magic* to talismans for various maladies according to the signs of the Zodiac - a very magical thing to do. This in addition to inventing an *Alphabet for the Magi*, used for engraving angelic names upon talismans.

Later on, following being virtually chased from Basel, he wandered the streets of Europe, Africa and Asia Minor in the search for hidden knowledge.

There has been some debate over the masculinity of Paracelsus. His skull was believed to have been in feminine proportions, he is never pictured with a beard and there was a tradition that he had suffered some form of accident during his childhood, which rendered him impotent.

According to a later colleague, Oporinus of Basel University, as a youngster, Paracelsus was tied up with a horse at a three-ways by his nurse who was sick of him. The horse then proceeded to emasculate the young boy. Whatever the truth, the event may reveal why Paracelsus was not overtly loving of the female sex.

There is also confusion, fostered by the Theosophist, Dr. Franz Hartmann, and others over his grandfather. The official biographies state that George Bombast had been a Grandmaster of the Teutonic Order – a Catholic Order with a diverse history. The Theosophists had it that George had been Grandmaster of the Knights of St. John, today known as the Sovereign Military Order of Malta, but no evidence backs this up.

At the age of twenty, Paracelsus travelled through Hungary and Germany, visiting mines and learning more about metals, gems and rocks. These were dangerous times for the young doctor and he records running from earthquakes, stone falls and floods and suffering from hunger, thirst and cataracts. He visited Russia and was taken captive by the Tartars who carried him to the great Khan, whom it appears he may have befriended – later travelling with the Khan's son on diplomatic work to Constantinople at the age of twenty-eight. It is then claimed that he learned the secret of the Philosopher's Stone from an unnamed Arabian, calling the prize Azoth. This Azoth was considered to be the universal cure-all and it's symbol the serpentine Caduceus. Paracelsus himself makes no

The single or double entwined serpent has been a symbol of healing for a long time

mention of this, in fact, and the only record comes from another alchemist known as Helmont (Jan Baptista van Helmont, 1580-1644). The fact remains however, that this long period in the lands of the East may not have only given him a unique insight into Arabian medical practices, but also the Eastern world of the Occult.

Following his time with the Tartars in Turkey, Paracelsus practiced medicine in the Italian Imperial Army, steadily growing a reputation as a great healer. All the time he gathered information, and marching with the Army the influence from across the regions was substantial. At the age of thirty-two he returned to Germany and assumed the title of medical doctor of both the internal and external, performing incredible acts of surgery relatively unseen in the West, but common in the East. His methods were at a tangent to the norm of Galen and even Hippocrates had not been translated, let alone read. In essence, his skills and success in healing, based outside of the norm and established methods was a threat to the existing infrastructure and right from the start tensions were high.

The existing methods dealt with the four temperaments or humors (choleric, melancholic, sanguine and phlegmatic), whereby human emotions were largely blamed for physical conditions and dealt with by venesection, purgation, vomiting and clysmata. With the spread across Europe of venereal disease, these ancient concepts were proving to be of no worth. One doctor, Jac Carpus of Bologne had tried and been successful in administering mercury to raise salivation - a secret he too had learned from Arabic sources on his journeys through Spain and Italy. Paracelsus had also learned of the use of mercury (which incidentally was also known as Azoth), according to some from Carpus himself, and prepared the medicine in pill form, thus achieving the same results, but in a much easier and gentler fashion than administering mercury. Using this same cure-all, Paracelsus claimed to cure leprosy, ulcers, gout and itching - all of which had been incurable under the Galenic method.

And so, Paracelsus grew in fame and fortune and the jealousy of his peers matched this growth. Nevertheless he was invited by the astutely political curators of Basel University to chair the professorship of medicine and philosophy. He accepted and pretty quickly insisted that the chemists and apothecaries should come under his watchful eye to ensure that they were preparing their goods to strict standards.

In addition to this shocking idea, at his very first lecture he solemnly burned the books of both Galen and Avicenna, claiming to have overcome them and that physicians should from that moment on, follow him.

In time, regardless of these bold statements, it is claimed that his lack of knowledge of Latin reduced his classes to almost nothing. I suspect that the powerful opposition he was stirring up also had a lot to do with it. Another professor, Oporinus, even accused him of being constantly drunk and after only three years Paracelsus quit.

The truth may be that Paracelsus did drink, water at the time was extremely dangerous and pretty much only alcohol was safe to drink. But now he was on the road again, staying at taverns and inns, curing people across the land. He proceeded to do this for the last four years of his life, dying at an Inn in Saltzburg – The Sign of the White Horse.

During his life, Paracelsus published only four books, and yet, following his death and the realization that his methods were actually more beneficial than previously thought, volumes of books attributed to him were released. In this way the actual beliefs and thoughts of Paracelsus himself have become clouded and obscured by those so-called adherents of the man himself. Not least of these was Oporinus, who had sat and listened to Paracelsus for three years and who later benefited from it by his copious printings. Oporinus claimed that one of the unknown cures was in fact opium, delivered up as small "mouse" pills and which would take away much pain. Although Oporinus seemed to have said many things against Paracelsus, he did in fact later defend his old tutor. In his work of nine books called *Archidoxa Medicinæ,* which contained the principles and maxims of the art, he stated, *"I intended to have published my ten books of* Archidoxa*; but finding mankind unworthy of such a treasure as the tenth, I keep it close, and have firmly resolved never to bring it thence, till you have all abjured* ARISTOTLE, AVICEN, *and* GALEN, *and have sworn allegiance to* PARACELSUS *alone."*

In the end, Paracelsus was proven to have been an excellent physician of his time. He gathered knowledge and information from across the known world and delivered it back to the people in their own language. As Gustav Bord said in his 1908 book, *La Franc-Maconnerie en France:*

"The doctrine of Paracelsus was drawn from the Cabala, Hermetic Philosophy and alchemy. He claimed to know and expound the entire system of the Mysterious forces which act in nature and man... Man must unite himself to the forces required in order to produce either physical or intellectual phenomena. The Universe was the Macrocosm, man was the Microcosm, and they were similar (as above, so below)..."

He countered the establishment, even if he did pay the cost when he had to flee Basel following the rise of the apothe-

The elderly Paracelsus, still no beard.

caries and others against his diatribe towards them. So what of his spiritual side that is clung to by the modern Theosophists? What was it that their virtual goddess, Madame Blavatsky so adored in Paracelsus?

In truth, it was the very fact that this physician was a precursor to Theosophy. He had gone into the East and brought back wonders and secrets lost, hidden and destroyed by the Western Catholic Church. He was heroic in this respect. They also saw other more esoteric aspects to Paracelsus within the few writings that can be attributed to him. To Blavatsky and others, these were deeply spiritual elements, but to the later psychoanalyst, Carl Jung, who lectured and wrote on Paracelsus, these were more in tune with modern psychology. What is the truth? To discover this, we have to visit the beliefs of Paracelsus and get inside his mind.

There is no doubt that Paracelsus believed in God and lived in a time when almost everybody did. This was a Christian God, a creator, filled with wonder, magic and mystery. Paracelsus said that everything that happens, does so via the Supreme and our very conscience comes to us because of God - and we ought therefore to follow it. Similar ideas we shall discover in the mind of the atheist H. G. Wells with regard to Nature. Indeed, Paracelsus said that he praised Nature and Nature praised him, for he came from Her and followed Her. He who wants to study the book of Nature, says Paracelsus, must wander with his feet over its leaves.

He backed Luther, and stood side by side with his wish to allow the masses the revelation of God. In fact even before Luther, Paracelsus had publicly burned a Papal bull at the same time he had burned the books of Galen and Avicenna. He loved wisdom and did all he could to gain more. In his book, *Paragranum* he said:

> "I went in search of my art, often incurring danger of life. I have not been ashamed to learn from that which seemed useful to me even from vagabonds, executioners, and barbers. We know that a lover will go a long way to meet the woman he adores; how much more will the lover of wisdom be tempted to go in search of his divine mistress!" *Lessico del Paragranum di Theophrast von |Hohenheim detto Paracelsus: I: indici.* Lessico Intellettuale Europeo XLVII, by Massimo Luigi. Bianchi, Edizioni dell'Ateneo, (1988)

For Paracelsus, the book of Nature was the one that all should read, especially those who wished to be physicians, for God himself had created Her. Which Temple holds the truth, he asked, those of the scholars such as Galen and Avicenna, or the Temple of Nature? He had a sense, derived from his more Eastern leanings, that all things were one, that man was no different in many respects to the Universe. To put it simply, the patterns of the heavens mirrored the patterns of man himself, we were in the image of God, the starry host. The Universal Mind or God is what would be called the upper firmament, the individual mind of man was the lower firmament. It was the knowledge of the upper, which gave rise to understanding the knowledge of the lower and vice-versa. This was very much part and parcel of Hermetic and esoteric lore and often imaged as the interlaced triangles, one pointing upwards and one downwards as in the Seal of Solomon. This was also the secret of astrology in a time when it was believed to open gateways to new and also ancient knowledge, and yet deemed sinful by the Church.

This unique concept is actually Gnostic. The true self is within each of us and is the point when we realize our connection to Nature itself. Until we understand that we are not separate from Nature we cannot discover Her or our true selves. Once we have connected to this natural source it was, and is, believed that the individual can know the secrets of Nature, for they will be one with Her. The adept will no longer need to seek out secrets in the world, for all answers will lay within. This kind of blasphemy and heresy was simply not accepted by the dogmatic Church.

Paracelsus said that he had reflected greatly on the magical powers of the soul of man and discovered the secrets of Nature. He said that only one who had undergone such training could become a true physician. All books could be burned, he said, and medicines thrown in the ocean for the mind in-tune with Nature no longer requires the physical substance, but instead perceives their goodness and recognizes the "signatum" – the signature or message the substance is wishing to relay to the body. In essence, there is a great deal of psychological healing at play in these statements – replacing miracle and religious healing with the power of thought. However there was more to his system. The "relationships" of the external world to the inner – the part needing healing – was profound to these people, who tried to discover correspondences between things. It was a perfectly logical thing to deduce. A few examples will help us understand by a sympathy between things. For instance, color was seen as being of incredible importance and each color had a corresponding star and plant or plants as well as curative power. Red was a stimulant, so find a red plant to stimulate the body, mind or senses; blue was soothing and good for the circulation of blood; yellow was poisonous and so was an excellent purgative. Various colored plants were found and prepared into medicines for use in the corresponding ailment. It was a little like discovering that water could put out a fire – it was a natural answer to a natural dilemma. Understanding and learning the correspondences between the anatomy of medicines and the anatomy of disease was the role of the physician and Paracelsus understood Nature so well that he almost intuitively discovered cures.

On the whole though, this remarkable synthesis between all things in the universe revealed to Paracelsus the hand of God and that was on the one hand, humbling, and on the other, empowering. He was humbled by the power of God and Nature and yet appeared to those who had no concept of this intuitive connection to nature as arrogant. Often our words can seem to get in the way of understanding and God is one of those words. I believe that God for Paracelsus was the ratio, mathematics, inspiration and energy behind existence. He was the architect behind all and so he was to be respected in that way. This energy of God, forming and destroying all things, forcing animal instincts as it forces planets to collide, was called by him the "soul". The soul-essence of man, or the energy, was formed by the planets, the plants, the sun – these things man fed upon and these things therefore man was, in the same way that a seed is not a Tree until it has fed from the soil, the sun and been given water. A tree is soil, water and solar energy and so too is man plant, animal, solar energy and water. Our connection to Nature is not just connection – we are Nature, but our consciousness has separated us from it. This is why Paracelsus had no worry about his home, his status, items or belongings. Nature was where his home lay.

All these same energies that make up man, animal and tree also make the Universe and so it reflects man, animal and tree and likewise they reflect it. By understanding this and the ratios of the energy (Golden Eye/Geometry) one could virtually predict what might happen, because it would be part of a pattern, which could be measured against the stars themselves. The power of this knowledge has been incredible. More than just being able to navigate well, man found his tools of benchmarking the planets would also aid him in the understanding of his very self – why, when and how he would do things. This was the kind of power that the occult driven elements of government were striving for during the Second World War. Adolf Hitler, Winston Churchill and a host of other leaders all had their own astrologers to aid in the prediction of human movement. Paracelsus was very close to powerful knowledge and there is little wonder that tradition has it he was murdered. This element of the occult, which simply means hidden from the eye, has been called magic for millennia. And just as the sleight of hand can fool the eye of the beholder who has no concept of how the trick is done, so too the knowledge of one who understands Nature and can predict outcomes from Natural Ratio, would also appear magical and hence we have religion. This is similar to the peculiar world that has risen around Paracelsus. Lack of understanding this ancient esoteric wisdom turned him into a witch, a charlatan, an alchemist and magician. He was none of these to those who understand, but he was all of them to those who are fools (i.e. in the old sense of the word), and it was this aspect which made him appear arrogant to a world of fools.

Man, said Paracelus, has the capacity to foresee future events and to read the future from the books of the past. The mystically inclined have taken this to mean that man can produce prophesy by slipping into some peculiar trance state, where in fact Paracelsus was simply making a statement of fact based upon man's connection to Nature. Man possesses the power to see friends thousands of miles away, by having this intuitive contact with the energy of the Universe. This was called the spiritual perception of man. It was the power of dreams in the waking state and those who did not have this power, this insight, were not in-tune. This Divine access was the reason Paracelsus did not desire books other than the word of God, for he could read Nature, in all likelihood took opium and believed he could access an incredible world-wide network of energy connection. These concepts were not new at this time and were in fact something that had been massively powerful for thousands of years, especially in the East. The Christian crusaders came into direct contact with these systems and entered a world of drug induced mysticism and Gnostic wisdom, bringing it back to Europe along with medicines, architecture and mathematics, where it lived under the shadow of Catholicism, hidden in alchemy until people such as Paracelsus and much later, Carl Jung, brought it to light again.

Paracelsus did not see anything wrong with all these systems, for as he himself said, he gained Wisdom, Reason and Knowledge from all things. Ignorance, he said, was the cause for imperfection and the imperfect man was thus because he was ignorant of his self and the light within. This light in the spirit of man illuminated everything for Paracelsus – it was the shining, the enlightenment, the illumination of countless generations that had gone before and that still today struggle to understand what is meant by it. Literally thousands of books and websites today are discussing this very human process as if it were something new and revealing a distinct duality no different to when Paracelsus attempted to explain it to his peers. One side sees in the trance spark a beautiful and enlightening experience of fulfillment and awakening for mankind. The other camp sees drug-induced hypnosis and self-delusion. The truth in fact, like most things, lays between those two statements.

Regardless of what one may think about Paracelsus and his beliefs we must remember the time in which he lived. He was a man of his time. He was one of those occasional stars that shine off and on as history plays out its passage. To look back from the 21st century and peer into the 16th with a judgmental mind would be wrong. Instead we should be simply looking to see what happened and to see what we can learn from it ourselves. If knowledge and learning does not make a better man out of me then it is of no worth. For me, Paracelsus was a confident and highly intelligent man who throughout his life wanted nothing more than to gain knowledge and wisdom by whatever means. What was the drive? Maybe it did have something to do with the lack of male genitals that tradition states and therefore he dedicated his life to healing? I suspect that the family background and the time in which he lived may have played a bigger role. Whatever the case, Paracelsus was a wise man and I leave him for the moment with a profound thought he offered to the world:

> 'The Will is a power hidden in the thought of man and becoming active through his imagination.'

Imagination is indeed a most powerful tool in the hands of a conscious human being as we shall learn in this book.

Chapter 2

Religion and Alchemists

In the introduction I spoke of control and the powers that administer this control. There are many organizations, groups, nations and religions that have attempted to gain control over the people and grow it via many methods. One of these is the Catholic Church, which to put it bluntly, began not as Jesus was taken from the cross, but as the fading Roman Empire clutched around for a new method of maintaining and growing power. It was understood that one did not need to own a country to control the mind of the people. Instead what was needed was control of the belief system - the very thing that answered the ultimate questions and problems of society. If you could re-write the various so-called Pagan religions of the globe into an all encompassing order then you were in with a good chance of succeeding. To add to this, very little evidence was required because not many people could read. For those who could, then the various texts were re-ordered and re-written to suit as many belief systems as possible.

In-order to spread the word of this newly formed amalgamated corporate machine the Church needed missionaries and so with the promise of salvation, food and employment thousands of priests were sent off around the world like sales representatives pushing a new vacuum cleaner. Over time the word of this new faith merged with local deities and old Pagan priests and Shaman became Catholic Priests. There were, however, those who would not listen or take up the cross and these had to be subdued in the name of Christ. Eventually Christianity grew for itself formidable armies from across Europe and the word turned into the sword.

This is the tale of one of those religious Orders that grew out of greed, hatred and envy, was based upon religious intolerance and yet managed to create such a myth of propaganda around itself that it was viewed as something of the highest spiritual and moral standing, and still is to this day.

This, however, is not a tale that will continue that propaganda. This is a work that will investigate the Order, warts and all, and reveal a startling conclusion that is simply ignored by most historians. Within this Order there were men who believed themselves to be great and are still held up as shining examples of good Christians. This Order attracted the rich and powerful and were responsible for fostering Christianity on the borders of Christendom. And yet, even within their ranks there was dissent and men who understood that the whole thing was a sham. At the very top of this uniquely focussed group emerged a man who delved deeper into the arcane world. He was a man who understood the role of the ruler and knew the secret world of Eastern esoteric philosophies; the powers of navigation and the wisdom of the healing arts. There are also men who use these elements of knowledge for their own selfish ends and all men are liable to fall short in the glory of God.

This is a history of the Sovereign Military Order of the Knights of Malta like you've never heard before. This is the tale of men of their time, who utilized the world around them to improve their physical, monetary and spiritual lot. These were not stupid men, these were individuals who recognized the times and lived according to it. Within this tale we will find two remarkable individuals, one from a poor background and one born in wealth, but both somehow are thrust together in the fight for self-glorification.

Many of the major problems we face in the world today can be traced back to one particular period in time. In the 11th century the Christian world was sent into a frenzy of religious bigotry and hatred towards all those who did not believe in Jesus Christ as the Savior of mankind. Hundreds of thousands of European Christian zealots poured across Europe, killing tens of thousands of Jews and other so-called unenlightened people along their way towards the battle grounds of the Holy Land.

This religious fervor had been created and fostered by the powers of the Roman Catholic, empire-building Church, over several decades. Gradually the message of peace and humility at the core of the original Christian teachings was eroded, amended and finally utterly destroyed in favor of a promise of salvation. Eternal life was offered for those who submitted themselves to the will of the almighty Church and offered their lives in combat against the evil Muslims. All the sins of your life and those of your ancestors would be forgiven if you took the cross and marched with your brethren into the Promised Land.

Over several decades subtle lies and myths were created

and fostered, surrounding the world of Islam, and Europe swallowed it completely. The Catholic Church utilized this emotional power, and the fear of hell, and went on a crusade to destroy its opponent, steal land and grow fat and rich on the proceeds. For too long the Catholic Church had failed to grow in wealth and military might because of its creeds, now it had all the tools it needed to turn this around.

The truth is that, on the whole, Christians, Jews, Gnostics and all-manner of other groups had lived relatively peacefully side-by-side with their Muslim rulers for 300 years. Islam saw them as the people of the book and Muslims were instructed to live in peace with them. The aggression came from the Christian side, spread originally by the Empirical Byzantine Church which was ignored initially by the Catholics, but then later utilized as a great story for their own ends. The Catholics, it seemed, were finally going to come running to aid their Byzantine brothers against the terrible onslaught of evil Islam. The truth was that both the Byzantine Church and Islam were in the sights of Western Europe and the war has been raging ever since.

History though is never quite so simple, for it involves humans who live with divided and often dualistic minds, cultures and civilizations. Islam is not free of blame and from early on in the 11th century there is evidence that some ill-treatment of Christian pilgrims occurred. One such event seems to have been a seed of much resentment.

Caliph Hakim was a Fatimite who was fanatical and demented. His rule was one of over zealous religious intolerance and culminated in his persecution of the Christians and the destruction of the Church of the Resurrection in Jerusalem in 1009. This kind of act played directly into the hands of a Catholic Church which had been steadily altering doctrine towards a more radical militaristic approach.

The stage was set for war between two powerful worlds.

Nevertheless a response did not come quickly and as problems continued in the Holy Land and propaganda built in the West the big confrontation had to wait until 1096 and 1097 as the First Crusade got underway in two waves.

It was in this period that the Order of St. John of Jerusalem was set up under the auspices of being a religious community to care for pilgrims. They were in fact originally part of the Benedictines, whose Patron Saint, John the Baptist they still

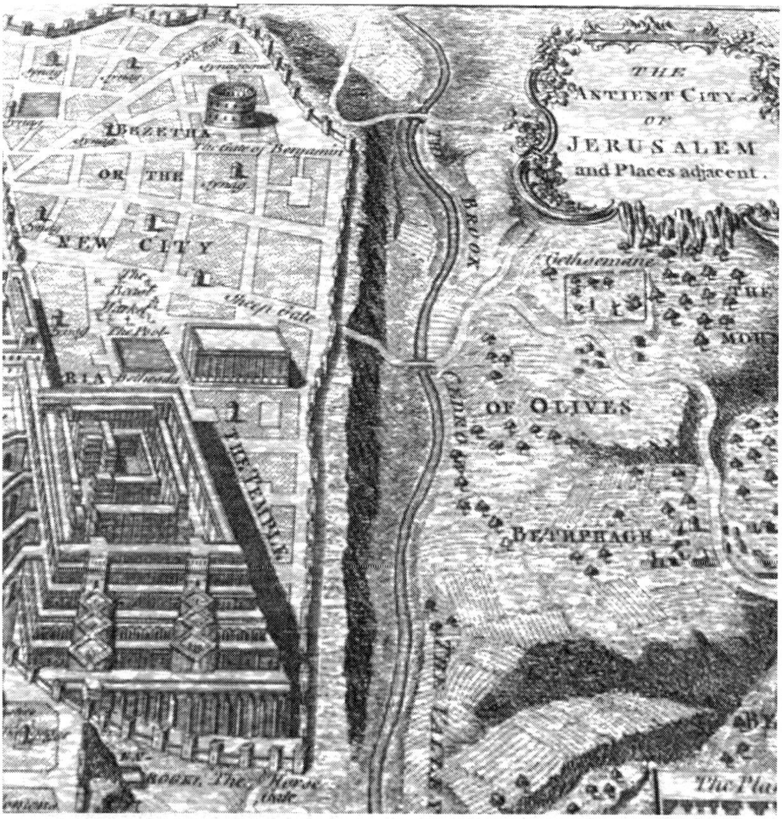

Jerusalem and the Temple.

revere. The very first Grand Master was brother Gerard who had in fact simply taken over the work of previous men and women such as Father Simon of Syracuse. The original location and acts of the Order therefore stretch back much further than the assumed date of 1099.

That they indeed cared for many Christians in those troubled lands is not doubted, whether they were in fact building underground networks of spies and undermining the social framework whilst doing so cannot be proven. However, the turn of events thereafter sees the Order building in importance and as Jerusalem fell to the Christians, their role increased and their rewards blossomed. By 1113 Pope Paschal II approved the foundation of their Hospital and placed the Order under the direct aegis of the Holy See, giving it virtual self-rule, apart from the interference of nation states.

The situation in the Holy Land quickly turned into a

European feudal battle-ground and the Order itself took on a military role due to the constitution of the King of Jerusalem and the rules of the new Grand Master, Raymond du Puy.

The Order, known commonly as the Knights Hospitallers, was now the defender of the faith as well as healer and mirrored their brothers in the Knights Templar, with whom they had some rivalry. It was at this early stage that the Order adopted the 8-pointed cross, known as the Amalfi cross, taken from Amalfi merchants who aided in funding the early hospice and made up of four arrows facing inwards.

By the end of the 13th century, the final Christian stronghold in the Holy Land fell and the Order retreated to Cyprus. Then in 1309 they took the island of Rhodes under the guidance of Grand Master Fulkes de Villaret. It was obvious to everybody by now that the defense of the West and the power of Christendom in the Mediterranean would rely heavily on a strong naval force and so the Order built one.

Soon the Order became renowned for its naval prowess, fighting many battles and aiding such Crusades as those in Syria and Egypt. Their skills helped not only the Christian and European cause, but also the Order itself as more and more

The Temple at Jerusalem, the seat of so much turmoil, but also sacred symbolism. It was here that the Knights of Malta began their rise.

rich and powerful Knights flocked from across the divided lands of Europe to join.

In addition to this, the Hospitallers took in the remnant of the disbanded and discredited Knights Templar, along with much of their treasure, wealth and land. Provence, Auvergne, France, Italy, Aragon, England, Germany and others all brought with them land and treasure, growing steadily the might of the Order. Governed by a Grand Master, the Order minted its own money, created its own rules and managed one of the most strategically powerful naval forces the planet had ever seen. And yet the pressure was still on and their military prowess made them a target for the Muslim, suffering several attempted invasions from the Sultan of Egypt and the Ottomans.

In 1522 the four hundred ships and two hundred thousand strong force of Suleiman the Magnificent finally arrived on Rhodes and there was a heroic six month siege ending in the Knights being allowed to respectfully withdraw to Sicily. It was a mistake Suleiman would regret.

For several years the Knights had no real home until they struck a deal with Emperor Charles V of Spain to occupy his islands of Malta and Gozo. Here the Knights grew in wealth and prestige and in 1565 they were to shock and amaze the known world by defending the islands valiantly against a massive Turkish invasion force.

Their constant actions against Barbary pirates and Muslim vessels had drawn the anger and focus of the Ottoman Empire. In addition to this, Malta itself was seen as essential for the Ottoman invasion of southern Europe. The only thing standing in the way were the Knights of Malta. Seven hundred Knights and around eight thousand soldiers were held back and defeated an estimated force of forty thousand Turks. Under the guidance of Grand Master Jean Parisot de la Valette, the Knights of Malta made a courageous stand against all odds and became the heroes of Christendom.

A new capital was now built, Valletta, and the ranks swelled. Honors poured in from across Royal Europe and the Knights loved it. Pride grew and for 200 years the Knights of Malta stood firm and sovereign over their land. They became fabulously wealthy and drew revenues from more than one hundred and forty estates in Palestine and from some nineteen thousand manors in Europe.

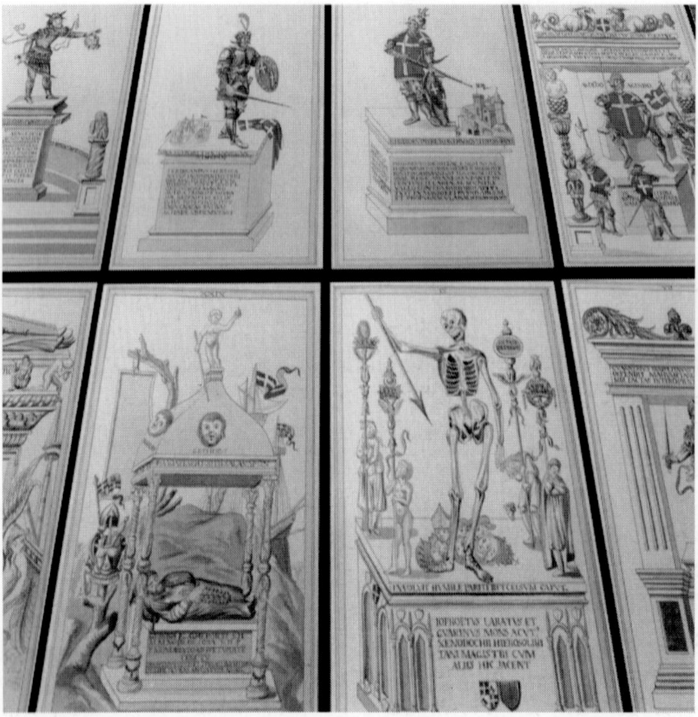

Incredible memorials placed upon the ground floor of several churches in Malta and Gozo.

The fantastic buildings of Malta and Gozo stand as a testament to the grandeur and power of the Order. They brought in the highest skilled artisans to create stunning works of art and fashion grand European buildings amongst some of the finest in the world. In their churches and Cathedrals they left behind beautiful marble memories of themselves with clever symbolic devices revealing many occult concepts and little in-jokes. Always mocking of death, which they believed to have overcome, these intricately crafted and designed concepts draw the visitor to stand in awe and compete with the over-powering size of the surrounding building and the masters artworks above.

And yet times were changing in the world, movements were forming, underground knowledge was being spread abroad and the old ways were falling apart. Royal houses collapsed, the power base of the Catholic Empire was being undermined and with it the power of the Order itself. Towards the end of their time in Malta the Grand Masters and

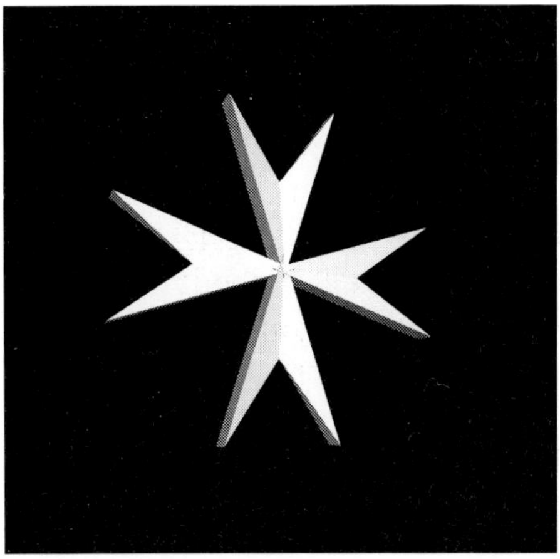

The Cross of Amalfi or the infamous Knights of Malta.

the Knights became something other than the supposed chivalrous and pure Knights of the Cross they were supposed to be. A rot set in, or even an enlightenment as some call it, bringing with it a new kind of renaissance Knight.

One of the final Grand Masters brought with him ideas outside of the Catholic creed and discredit on the Order itself. His name was Manuel Pinto da Fonseca.

Pinto

It is the mid 18th century and the grand city of Valletta is the pride of Malta. Outside St John's Church there is a throng of people awaiting word on the new Grand Master who would lead them. The clouds begin to break up and the sun shines through - a good omen is claimed by the masses - God has spoken.

The announcement is swiftly made, the new Grand Master will be Portuguese, his name Manoel Pinto de Fonseca, known later by all as Grand Master Pinto.

The people are overjoyed and live in hope that this will be an upright and honest leader. Pinto had, after all been Vice-Chancellor to Grand Master Vilhena, a highly respected man and it is hoped that Pinto learned much from his time as underling. These hopes will soon be dashed. Pinto was the 68th Grand Master of the Order of the Holy Religion of the Knights of St John of Jerusalem, of Palestine, of Rhodes and Malta. He reigned from 1741 to 1773.

Very swiftly Pinto set to work attempting to overcome the problems he had inherited, mainly the rapidly emptying coffers of the Order. He began by raising a loan and set about several building campaigns, not least of which was to be a city named after himself, but which eventually took the title of Qormi. He also attempted to begin cultivating silk by planting mulberry trees but failed miserably. What surprised everybody though was how he pressed new coins to celebrate every single new venture, no matter how small. Nobody could figure out why, other than the assumed arrogance of Pinto himself and his desire to be remembered by posterity.

Indeed, this was the pattern Pinto was to set for most of his reign and it drew the consternation of his Knights and the people of Malta ultimately to the point of revolution. In 1749 one of his bodyguards named Cassar, discovered a Turkish plot lead by a Muslim slave named Mustafa Pasha, to overthrow Pinto. The plot was halted, the ring leaders punished and Pinto pressed more coins to celebrate. However, Mustapha was an incredibly important slave, being the Pasha of Rhodes and under French pressure and for peace with the Turks Pinto released him.

In his zeal to become something almost secular, Pinto began creating new titles for his nobles and indeed himself. He became Most Eminent Highness and called himself Prince of Malta. His prestige amongst the nobles of Europe grew and grew. He built universities, hospitals, courts of justice and improved the defenses.

The austere look of a man who is extremely confident.

The Knights of Malta were certainly no longer mere monks and servants of the Pope, they had ideas far in excess of their little rocky island in the Mediterranean. Pinto knew and understood the power he had in this rapidly changing world - that he was the sovereign of a very strategically placed island, that he and his men stood between the East and the West. His Knights were in fact some of the world's most powerful nobles or sons of nobles, collected from across Europe. And he also knew that this strength would depend upon his own clever chess playing and he played non-stop, with monarchs across Europe.

Pinto was political, not religious. His power was in his prestige and position, not in his humility to the Church. He knew that times had changed and with it the Order itself was under threat. Europe was no longer predominately Catholic and trouble in France would slow the massive revenue from the French knights. His own Maltese subjects were turning on him due to the revolutionary ideals spreading rapidly around the world and the falling standard of living on the islands. All men are equal was the call of the common man and yet, Pinto maintained a pompous and austere profile, lavishing luxuries on himself and his friends.

His attitude drew the attention of the islands religious authorities and so he took them head on. Pinto's opinion was that the religious leaders were fostering the antagonistic view of the people and he decided to manipulate the situation. He could not touch the Bishop and even less the island's Inquisition, without major upset and probably his own unseating, but he could fight the Catholic spy network - the Jesuits.

In truth the Knights of Malta and the Jesuits had never seen eye to eye and many believed that the Jesuits had become too powerful in the Order itself. In addition there was also the very wealthy Jesuit College and Pinto had his eye on it.

However, only the Pope himself could remove the Jesuits from Malta and so Pinto fabricated a lie that it was in fact the King of Prussia, Frederick II, who was demanding their expulsion. Even though the Pope knew of the lie, the request was granted and the Jesuits expelled in 1768.

Following a powerful battle between Pinto and the Inquisition for the Jesuit College, Malta emerged with its own University and Pinto seemingly more arrogant than ever.

So what is the truth? Was Grand Master Pinto simply a man caught between two worlds? The old religious and monarchical orders and the new power of the people? Was he trying to bridge the divide on Malta? Or was he simply fighting for the survival of the Order and perpetuating the memory of his own rule?

The truth is that Pinto, like many Knights and Grand Masters before him, did not follow the rules of religious convention. They were not entirely pious, they gambled, battled and fornicated like all men. Pinto himself had an illegitimate son named Jose Antonio Pinto de Fonseca e Vilhena. The line still exists to this day.

In fact, the Knights of Malta have not been entirely truthful or forthcoming in regard to their darker historical secrets and we may find that nothing has changed. One dark secret however, which caused a scandal for Pinto himself was the affair of the alchemist and the Order.

Cagliostro

Since the medieval period and before, great minds in Europe had known that there was more knowledge in the world than that passed on to them by the rule of the Church. They knew that the fables of Christianity were employed by those in power to maintain and build that power. And so many searched out that hidden and sometimes lost knowledge and built great libraries of occult wisdom.

These men and women were not ordinary men and women, they were learned in the arts, languages, sciences and politics. Neither were they alone in their drive to uncover ancient secrets. Often societies and organizations grew up around them and today we have the vestiges of these early groups in the Freemasons, Rosicrucians and others. These were powerful people, very often within the heart of government. People such as Dr. John Dee in Elizabethan England held great power over those around him for his own personal knowledge and his collection of books.

By the late 18th century the Freemasons had become one of the most powerful none-state, non-religious and non-governmental bodies in the known world and it was spreading like wild-fire. To curb this power the Catholic authorities banned it outright, and yet it crept abroad unabated and spread even

Freemasonry crept into the Knights of Malta from a very early date, along with it came Cagliostro.

within the Catholic fold, making a mockery of the ban, as it still does to this day.

The very basis of Freemasonry reveals a knowledge that is not just claimed to be from before the advent of Christianity, but was in fact based upon the knowledge that created Christianity. The Knights of Malta, under the leadership of Grand Master Pinto, were not separated from this influence – an influence, which was aiding in the spread of the overthrow of monarchies and religious power and spreading the word of equality for all mankind. Whilst disseminating these new world views, Freemasonry was in fact being joined and taken over itself, by the very people it supposedly sought to undermine. In truth, these new movements simply shifted the power base back to the old elite, whilst circumnavigating the emotional tide of the masses.

One man who helped in the spread of this relatively new movement and who would scandalously come into contact with the Knights of Malta is known as Count Alessandro Cagliostro and his own history is clouded in mystery and intrigue.

It is claimed that Cagliostro's real name was Guiseppe Balsamo and by others that this is itself a fabrication. Evidence from 1787 uncovered by Goethe (writer, philosopher and diplomat, 1749-1832) and closer to the period than anybody else, reveals documents placing Cagliostro's heritage within the Balsamo family and Goethe even visited Felicita Balsamo, Cagliostro's mother, in Palermo to ascertain the truth. The evidence however still remains very weak.

For himself, Cagliostro claimed to have been born of Christians of noble birth and abandoned at birth on the island of Malta, but no other evidence backs up this claim, which was in all likelihood used as a means of accessing the Knights of Malta and various other dignitaries. The claim in fact becomes more bizarre, mystical and builds his occult pedigree as he supposedly travels to Medina, Mecca and Cairo, learning the sacred arts of alchemy, the cabala and magic.

In truth, he appears to have been given a perfectly good education in Palermo, Sicily, nearby Malta and to have become a novice in the Catholic Order of St. John of God, from which he was soon expelled. However he did learn chemistry and the almost magical spiritual rites that he would later adapt.

Fleeing to Messina, following some dubious attempts at fraud, we next find Cagliostro on the island of Malta and here we know the history to be true, for it is recorded by the Knights themselves. Here Cagliostro became an auxiliary of the Order, using his medical and chemistry skills as a pharmacist within the hospital. The lessons he learned whilst in the Order would later be put to great use in the Royal courts of Europe, where this great magician and alchemist would reveal healing works of wonder.

The later archivist of Grand Master Rohan would write that Pinto spent one million lire in entertaining Cagliostro, an incredible sum of money for a fraudulent drop-out at anytime. There had to be good reason.

The Knights of Malta were duty bound by statute to avoid such unsavory characters and even in cosmopolitan Valletta they were instructed to shy away from the influx of adventurers walking the streets. And yet, Grand Master Pinto, the very head of the same Order broke this rule in style with one of the most infamous characters of the century.

The diary of Saverio Mifsud, a Maltese doctor of the time, reveals the truth:

> "For some months there had been lodging in the Palace of His Most Serene Highness, a man who claims to be a chemist. This man was received by his aforementioned Highness and admitted to his full confidence, being lodged in his Palace and maintained at his own expense. The reason for this is that he has announced his intention to concoct a certain elixir of life designed to keep man sound in health both in body and mind." Saverio Mifsud, "Egregie Doctor", 1842, Hill Museum and Manuscript Library, Malta.

Why Pinto associated with this strange fraudster is not entirely known, but the truth probably lies in Pinto's own fascination with alchemy. In taking Cagliostro into the very heart of his palace, Pinto went against the rules of the Order, but in his own open fascination with alchemy, even turning over rooms in his own palace for the work, simply went against the rules of the Church. Pinto was openly his own man and sought out greater knowledge.

Whether Cagliostro and Pinto actually managed to uncover the secret of the elixir of life is open to debate, but Grand Master Pinto was the longest lived of all Grand Masters, dying at the incredible age of 92 and being perfectly lucid until the end - fit indeed of body and mind.

One symbol that always surfaces in the work of alchemists and mystics is that of the serpent and in Malta this symbol is to be found on almost every religious building in one form or another. The official story has it that this was because St. Paul supposedly survived a snake bite when he landed upon the island and this itself is a cover story for an arcane truth as I have shown in my previous works. There are several reasons for the use of snakes as symbols and each one has merit depending upon the period, location and subject of the use. Often the serpent is a symbol of the perceived internal energy or spirit that Shaman and mystics have for thousands of years professed to seeing in their visions. Another reason is that energy itself is a wave-form, that it appears in nature as a wave and man has utilized several methods of revealing this hidden serpent. Smoke, sand and water have all been found by archaeologists to have been used for such a purpose. Another good reason for the symbol of the serpent is the very natural phenomenon of the snake sloughing off it's skin. It appears to die and resurrect, leaving behind it's shroud, which became sacred. While researching *The Serpent Grail,* I also discovered that the venom of the snake was, and is, used as a form of elixir due to its high protein content. Symbolically, the snake was used to indicate balance and wisdom – the fiery serpent and the watery serpent being used as symbols of emotion and logic and various other human traits which need constant balancing. In alchemy, the serpent has several purposes and involve the unifying and mixing processes. All these and more, are good reasons for the use of the serpent in symbolism and in each case we have to be careful regarding the period and location as to which one may be the reason for the symbolic use. We should also be aware, that very often all elements of our story do in fact tie together. The Druid was a priest, a master over the people, he was also the architect or "mason", with the power of rule and measure. As the prophet of the clan he foretold the future and called himself the serpent.

What is interesting to note in the tale of Cagliostro however is the very symbol with which he identified himself known as the Seal of Cagliostro.

This unusual symbol depicts a serpent, an apple in its mouth, impaled with an arrow and was found amongst his personal effects upon his death in 1795. While the symbol has obvious alchemical elements, its precise meaning is unknown although the great mystical writer, and Freemason, Eliphas Levi, stated that it contained the names Acharat and Althotas, two names associated with Cagliostro and representing the Great secret and the Great work of the alchemist. It is in fact the symbol of union between the opposing forces – the universal balance, which is the great work itself – upon the self.

Using his new-found friends in high places Cagliostro, however, moved on to Rome where he worked for a short time for Cardinal Orsini, whilst continuing to sell magical amulets and even producing forgeries. He married and moved to London, Russia, Germany and later France amongst other countries where he helped to spread his Egyptian Rite of

Freemasonry, meeting such great men as Benjamin Franklin. The ancient knowledge of balance and self-discovery of the God within was a message that once again found fruit amongst the great thinkers of the world - in fact leading to what was termed eternal life, and thus the true elixir of life, that of the power of the serpent symbol, - the balance of the mind with the deity within.

In France he was prosecuted in the scandalous affair of the diamond necklace, which involved Marie Antoinette and Cardinal Rohan, but was later released due to insufficient evidence against him. Nevertheless he was asked to leave France and arrived in England where he was forced to deny charges of being an ordinary commoner and not of noble birth at all - denying that he was Guiseppe Balsamo in an open letter to the English people.

Eventually Cagliostro visited Rome where he was caught red-handed as a fraudster by spies of the Inquisition and probably betrayed by his own wife. He was sentenced to death, which was later revoked to life imprisonment and died in the Fortress of San Leo.

For all his faults, Cagliostro made his mark supplying the supposed mystery of the ancients to the hungry minds of the Royal courts in Europe and all this following his time with the Grand Master of Malta. Going strictly against the Orders own rules which state:

> 'No one should dare to practice any kind of sorcery, or be involved in it, or imitate any form of it; anyone found guilty of practicing any of these sorceries, or commissioning such practices to others, will be condemned to row on the galleys for five years. The same punishment will be meted out to those goldsmiths and silversmiths who dare receive or work any kind of metal for alchemy, without earning any exemption of the penalty on the plea of ignorance.'

Grand Master Pinto was in fact not just interested in the world of the occult, he actually lead a secret enclave of twenty-three specially chosen noblemen from across Europe. These special people were in Malta for the purpose of discovering the secret of the Philosopher's Stone itself, understanding the cabala and getting to grips with divination. Cagliostro was simply brought in to offer up his own knowledge and in doing so learned much more himself. He moved on throughout

Europe and spread the new word. The underground survival of the Order would continue in the rites of the Order within the Freemasons themselves.

Evidence from two Scottish travelers, William Baird and Ian Douglas, in around 1770 shows Grand Master Pinto presiding over this circle of magic and confirming that Cagliostro was in fact receiving an education at the hands of the Knights themselves, even though Pinto had stated that Cagliostro was a fraud.

Baird claims the Grand Master said:

> 'When you leave this isle, you will be skilled and skilful and very formidable practitioners of the hermetic arts. Nothing happens by accident, except disasters. If you are here tonight, it is because you were drawn by that great emanation of God that attracts all who desire wisdom. It is because of willingness to learn that you have been chosen to receive the teachings of the most benevolent wizards of yore. Over the next few years all of your questions will be answered.... When you leave Malta you will understand why events happen or not. You will be able to shape happenings toward the good of humanity.' Secrets of Malta, by Virginia M. Fellows, Gnosis Magazine No.40 (Summer 1996).

According to Baird, this new secret society, founded by Pinto, Cagliostro and the infamous St. Germain was threatened by the later Illuminati of Adam Weishaupt, even though Cagliostro admitted under oath to also be a member of the same group. The truth is that Baird's entire work cannot be trusted and has been shown to be flawed in several areas. The underlying thesis, however, holds water when one looks at the facts. Pinto did have an alchemy lab, he did draw in close brothers from across Europe, he did take in Cagliostro and aid in the spread of Egyptian Freemasonry. Other elements of the text, in the possession of John Baird, one of the travelers descendents, reveals that Pinto was involved in the Eastern practices very similar to the adepts of later times and of whom we shall speak in the chapter on Bram Stoker. These practices involved the light sheath or the astral body and the processes known by many today as the Kundalini – the serpent energy of the light body. As these ancient secrets spread across Europe, re-awakening the very same concepts once worshipped world-wide, they took on a sinister role in the Christian mindset.

Maltese folktales also back the myths, especially the feeling among the locals that Pinto was some kind of strange vampire, living to an old age and practicing peculiar magic rituals. Baird may well have been reporting on perceived truths and revealing emotions that were based in certain facts. It was even later reported that Cagliostro had been the illegitimate son of Pinto himself.

The facts that we do have show strange meetings, scandalous affairs with alchemy and the occult, the spreading of illegal secret societies, an underground knowledge and the drawing close of an old power system. The question, on a perfectly political front, now has to be, just how and why did the Knights of Malta survive and indeed obtain permanent observer status within the world's most powerful group of countries - the United Nations?

The Modern Era of the Knights

Today, entry to the original Knights of Malta is as closed to the ordinary man as it ever was. Yes, there are numerous modern re-inventions all claiming to be somehow linked to the Order, but they are not. The true Order remains today the Sovereign Military Order of Malta and is a closed Roman Catholic fraternity, allowing only those of noble birth entry into their inner most ranks.

The sovereign Grand Master is recognized by nations around the world as a head of State, given religious rule with the title of Cardinal and secular power with the title of Prince, even though there is no land to rule over. Their land is one unseen.

Members owe allegiance to their leader as a royal head of State and this being above the land of their own birth. Evidence of their power is found just after the Second World War when their ability to issue passports enabled them to aid Nazi's fleeing mainland Europe with false identities. Indeed they issued their highest reward, the Grand Cross of Merit, to the Nazi General Reinhard Gehlen.

It is claimed by conspiracy researchers across the world that the Knights have been implicated in the construction of the CIA and even Watergate journalist, Carl Bernstein, claimed

The Templars may be world famous for all-manner of reasons, but the Knights of Malta also hold their own mysteries.

that Ronald Reagan's CIA director, William Casey was a Knight and gave secret information to Pope John Paul II. Their main aim to reduce the power of communism.

In fact, following the Second World War, Nazi, Catholic and the Western World joined forces against the rise of communism, which threatened to undermine the very power of each and every European State and there was little evidence that it would end there. There is little wonder therefore that the Knights, all men of considerable power and authority, were involved in joining forces with the Office of Strategic Studies, the SS, the British Secret Service and other Catholic powers to fight the power of communism. Part of this battle included recruiting and redirecting ex-Nazi war criminals as early spies and fighters against the Russian threat. The effective use of the Order's passports was simply part of this secret work.

From the secretive Bilderbergers to the Freemasons, from the CIA to MI5, the Knights of Malta were and can be found. The reason is simple. It is because they are men of noble birth, who are taught and trained in the highest schools and universities in the world and that enter politics and positions of power unlike almost any other closed society. Because of this their lives are scrutinized by conspiracy buffs and implicated in almost every scandalous affair on record.

The question has to be asked though, is it fair and right that those born into families that are wealthy and powerful should tell the rest of the world how to live? Are we right to leave the massive international games to these few men who have their base in the Vatican? What in fact, is their goal?

There are approximately now 11,000 Knights world-wide, with many break-off groups including the protestant Order in Great Britain closely associated and technically having allegiance to the Pope via the ruling monarch. This Order also now has membership of the United Nations, even though it technically has no nation. Why should these people have such access to this incredible power? Did you vote for them?

Islamist fundamentals have called for the destruction of the Knights Embassy in Egypt claiming that the Knights are continuing in their sacred pledge to destroy Islam.

"Do not stint in your attacks" they say "I ask Allah to have it closed down or blown up."

The age of the internet and the dissemination of information has made it possible to join the dots, and together with conspiracy theorists, these Islamic terrorists have worked out that certain members of the Knights Order are also implicated in the security firm, Blackwater, which has been used by the USA military to protect its personnel in the various wars.

Whether it is communism or Islam from the East, the capitalist and royalist system of the Catholic West is in stark contrast to the concepts of equality under the divine or the proletariat. The battle line was drawn many centuries ago, a division of idealism, and neither side is so right that it should cause war and suffering on any scale. Man does not have the divine right to rule over another, nor does he have the power to overcome his own greed in a communist State. Both ideals are flawed and a new, third way needs to be found if we are to stop this thousand-year-old war.

No matter what opinion one may have of the war between West and East, Christianity and Islam, Capitalism and Communism, it appears to still be raging and it appears that the warriors of Christ in the black cloak and white cross are still fighting it.

We should do well to remember the words from the start of this work:

> "This religious fervor had been created and fostered by the powers of the Catholic Empire-building Church over several decades. Gradually the message of peace and humility at the core of the original Christian teachings was eroded, amended and finally utterly destroyed in favor of a promise of salvation. Eternal life was offered for those who submitted themselves to the will of the almighty Church and offered their lives in combat against the evil Muslims."

Chapter 3

H. G. Wells – The Man on the Moon

We have seen how one religious Order and several men within it can influence society. They can, under the radar of their own religion, spread and disseminate ideas and concepts that are not only alien to their own stated beliefs, but also against the very rule of Mother Church. Within the Knights of Malta an ancient belief system was fostered, taught and spread – injecting afresh the ancient ideas within alchemy of Gnosis and Eastern psychological processes at a time that was rife for it. Each time has a moment awaiting that spark, that re-awakening and Europe was ready for the revival of philosophies that had been hidden, destroyed and made to appear evil.

Cagliostro, Paracelsus, Pinto, St Germain and many others have all left their mark in history. Today these individuals would be very different, but in their own time they managed to make some kind of difference, however we view that with modern eyes. What was their purpose? Did they have a long-term view of society? And were they attempting to change it? Or were they simply living their lives in their own time, fascinated with concepts that seemed more dangerous and intellectual than the Sunday School mantras of their masters?

There are some men who leave a mark on society so large that it remains forever. H. G. Wells is one of these. He may not have saved humanity by discovering a new cure for cancer

The man himself, portraying that confident look he was famous for.

and he certainly didn't impressed those around him with his chivalrous attitude, but he did influence the entire world through his science fiction novels and possibly a great deal more than any of us realize.

Born on the 21st of September 1866, Herbert George Wells was the fourth child of Joseph Wells and Sarah Neal. He was born into a class of people known as the lower middle-class, who had to work hard for a living and yet also had certain privileges such as schooling. They were poor people and Joseph Wells had to work selling bats and balls at cricket matches to survive.

When he was only seven years old, H. G. Wells broke his leg and was confined to his bed where he spent many hours reading books from the local library. He read of other worlds and places and dreamed of writing his own fantastic works. Upon his recovery he attended Morley's Commercial Academy where he learned useful skills such as sums and writing, but when his father had an accident and the income dried up he was forced to take up an apprenticeship at the Southsea Drapery Emporium. This was an incredibly boring and frustrating period for this creative young man and yet he later turned the period to his advantage by retelling elements of his time there in two popular books – *The Wheels of Chance* and *Kipps*.

It was around this period that his mother and father began to live separate lives, although they never actually divorced. For Wells himself, marital bliss and devotion to one woman would be a difficult task and one he would fail at. He also failed utterly as a drapers apprentice, and then a chemists' assistant and even as a teacher's aid. Each time he would return to his mother at Uppark Country House in Sussex where he immersed himself in the wonderful library.

Eventually Wells won a scholarship at what would become the Royal College of Science in London and he studied biology under T. H. Huxley, grandfather of Aldous Huxley. During his time here he had been on the debating circuit and met with members of the socialist Fabian Society – both crucial elements in forming the mind of the later Wells. However, when he left school he was penniless and went to stay with his Aunt Mary, where he met and fell in love with his cousin, Isabel. They married in 1891 and Wells taught for a living, where he then met and fell in love with a student, Amy Catherine

Robbins (also known as Jane), whom he then married in 1895 following his divorce from his cousin.

H. G. Wells had a wandering eye for the ladies and had several affairs including Margaret Sanger, the American activist, writer Amber Reeves, novelist Rebecca West, Odette Keun and Russian spy Moura Budberg. His wife, Amy, knew all about these illicit liaisons and even the children that resulted, but nevertheless remained his wife until her own death in 1927.

Wells had been writing almost the whole time and not always upon subjects of science fiction. His stories were very often commentaries on society and, in 1895, he managed to have several of his tales published; the first being *Select Conversations with an Uncle,* followed quickly by the classic *Time Machine*. By 1897 *The Invisible Man* was published and, in 1901, *The First Men on the Moon.*

By 1902 the socialist mind of H. G. Wells led him to join the Fabian Society, although later when he argued with another writer, George Bernard Shaw, he resigned.

His ideas were growing in strength the whole time and concepts of a new world order were emerging. In 1905 he wrote *A Modern Utopia* in which he proposes a world-wide state wherein everybody would live a happy life. This work was really his first foray into what would become his ideal of a new world order and is a mixture of fiction and fact. Man, claimed Wells, would look and appear the same in this Utopian society, but his attitudes would change. He would work towards the goals and aspirations of all, and not the individual. The money of this new world would be gold coins of a fair size. On the one side the lion of strength and power and the other the "goddess" of peace and justice – a distinctly Manichean approach without the need for the religion of Mani.

Wells also reveals in this book his feminist devotion – that women are equals to men and require respect. Considering the love of his mother and the aid of his aunt, the upbringing of Wells must surely have had some influence here. Indeed Wells makes the point that motherhood is as good a career as any in the male dominated arena.

A prolific writer, he continued to create works of both fact and fiction, commenting all the time, whether openly or not, upon the perils of our society and the need to change it. He traveled extensively and even visited Communist Russia, providing an excellent report for the West on the conditions and beliefs of her people - albeit in rather rose-tinted socialist gloss.

Wells was becoming an international celebrity and his comments were not taken lightly. He wrote histories of the world and even collaborated with Sir Julian Huxley and his own biologist son, George P Wells on *The Science of Life*.

By 1933 he had written the classic and prophetic *The Shape of Things to Come* in which he speculates, using fiction, on the way the world will develop from 1933 to 2106. There are visions of mass destruction by flying machines and the coming one world state he himself envisioned. This Utopia of Wells has everybody speaking English, the promotion of science and the eradication of religion entirely.

In 1939 he follows up with the timely *The Holy Terror*, in which he details the traits of the world's fascist dictators, such as Stalin, Mussolini and Hitler. In January of 1940 he published *The New World Order*, which today is heralded as the Illuminati handbook of world domination by conspiracy theorists across the world. In fact this is a very clever socialist work, explaining how he believed that a one world government would in fact bring peace and stability into a world of warfare. Admittedly Wells makes no mistake in understanding that not everybody will like the idea, but insists that regardless, the new world order must arise, and that each and everyone of us must change our ways in order for this to be accomplished.

The symbol of communism – a little known fact that Wells visited Russia and reported on his findings.

The notoriety of H. G. Wells was greatly enhanced when Orson Welles produced the Mercury Theatre radio adaptation of *The War of the Worlds* in 1938. The broadcast was so realistic that widespread panic ensued. People ran out into the streets dressed only in towels and congregations of Christians begged God for mercy.

The terror and confusion caused by the broadcast so shocked Orson Welles that he publicly apologized and promised never to do it again. At the time, H. G. Wells was not at all amused by the situation, but only two years later he calmed down and even helped Orson Welles advertise his classic film, *Citizen Kane*.

During the Second World War, Wells lived in his house in Regent's Park, London and published his last book, *Mind at the End of its Tether* in 1945, yet another critique of society with his usual pessimistic outlook on humanity. He died in London on August the 13th, 1946.

The War of the Worlds

Perhaps the most widely known work of H. G. Wells is *The War of the Worlds,* along with *The Time Machine* and *The Invisible Man.* Although each book deals with contemporary society, for me the most profound is *The War of the Worlds*. When Wells writes about society in general he is mainly pessimistic, claiming that humanity is rushing towards catastrophe and that mankind needs to wake up and change things.

The War of the Worlds, for those who have not seen any of the films or read the book, is the tale of a Martian invasion of Earth, centered in the narrative around London. The Martians almost immediately begin to harvest humans, encroaching upon the earth like a swarm of locusts. The military throw their might at the advanced technology but to no avail and all hope seems lost. Humanity, it seems, is not as advanced or clever as it once believed and the realization of this fact is difficult for people to come to terms with. Even, and especially, religion is of no use, as the character of the curate breaks down in fear – his false belief system cannot save him when it comes to the crunch.

Here, the evolutionary beliefs of Wells are coming through loud and clear. The scientific knowledge and beliefs, and his background in biology are put to good use as he makes the point that nature can be brutal in its race to survive. One

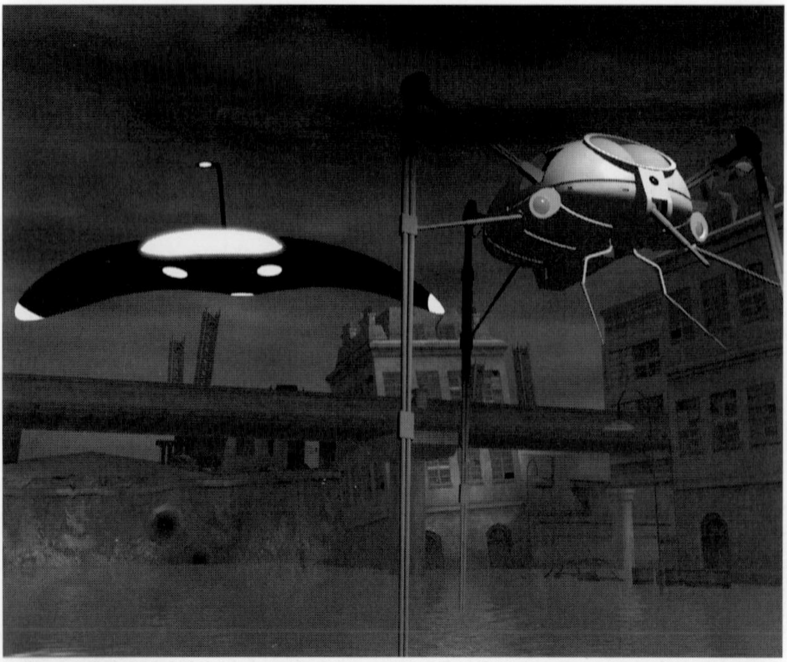

War of the Worlds is probably one of H. G. Wells's most famous tales, but what does it mean?

species will devour another and the strongest shall win the day. Wells also understands that nature has a unique ratio built in of beautiful balance and the life-forms of the planet earth fight back. In this case it is a pathogenic bacteria that silently destroys the aliens and saves the human race. The earth is back in balance, for now.

Wells knew, and stated as such, that the human population of the globe would reach a point when nature would re-balance itself and reduce the human race back down to a sustainable level. He was also fully aware that society in general operated as a mirror to these same principles and so *The War of the Worlds* is also a political and social statement of the period in which he lived. Mankind, he says, is not prepared for invasion of such magnitude because it does not act as one. Just as the nations of Europe were divided in the Middle Ages and so failed to operate as one fighting army in the Crusades, so today the nations of the world are divided and unable to work together for the greater good of the species. This is invasion literature of the highest order and as we shall see in the novel *Dracula* by Bram Stoker it was a popular underlying subject matter of the period delivering the stark message "beware nations of the West, there are forces that would overcome you, but they are not necessarily always earthly."

There is no point in turning to the military, no reason to cry out to God and panic and terror will get you nowhere, says Wells. (Is this a quotation? Nope it's an analysis of his mind) You were not prepared in the first place and you are fortunate to be part of nature this time, but beware of her power, for she is the ultimate force in the universe.

The Time Machine

The Time Machine is a remarkable book on many levels. It is psychologically intuitive, giving us an insight into Wells perception of each time frame and how man reacts according to his time. It is prophetic, in that it makes clever technological and social predictions, many of which, like Wells' other works, have come true.

Published in 1895, it is one of his earlier works and reveals that he was already well-aware of the catastrophic mind of the human psyche when out of tune with nature. It is also the very

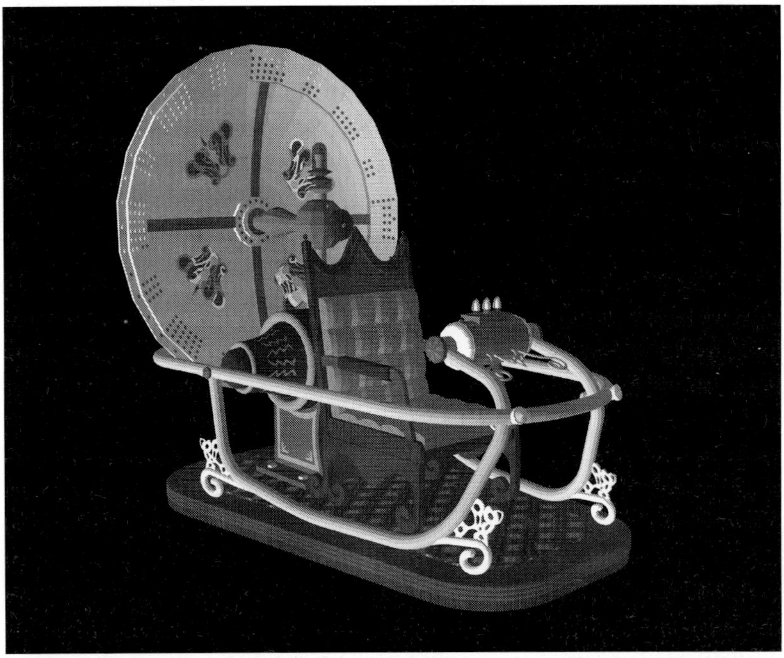

Who has not heard of the famous machine that can travel through time, what message does each new period hold for us?

first use of the phrase "time machine", which has been used by almost everybody since for such a device.

In the book we find our Time Traveler, who is unnamed and thus everyman, travelling to the year 802,701 where he finds a perfectly peaceful and communist community who call themselves the Eloi. The word is actually Aramaic and means "my God" and may be a religious jibe on Wells' part.

The Eloi live above ground and appear almost Hobbit-like being only four-feet tall with pink skin and large eyes. They are child-like and seem to have no cares in the world. There is no industry and no infrastructure and the Traveler is obviously confused at this peculiar state when he discovers that this harmonious utopia is actually a deceit.

Beneath ground live the Morlocks who toil to keep the machines working that, in-turn, keeps their flock of Eloi happy and peaceful above ground. In fact the Eloi are food for the Morlocks who are cannibals. This is a continuation and caricature of the class system that Wells himself was utterly against. He did not believe that one part of society should feed off another, but that a more communist style of living should pervade. Here, Wells is stating that nothing has changed and that our very natures force this to come out. In the future our very physical forms will evolve according to our systems of society. The Morlocks are those who have power and wealth at the expense of the working classes who are the Eloi. So much for "your God" is Wells' statement.

Eventually the Traveler escapes the Morlocks and shoots off into the future more than 30 million years. He watches as the earth, without life other than lichens, decays. In the end, Wells is making the point that our struggles against each other are pointless, the power of the universe, of nature itself is more than we realize.

Beliefs

Similar themes on society and religion, on nature and the mind of man are to be found in many of the works of H.G. Wells, whether fact or fiction. His distinctly anti-Christian writings brought down the consternation of such famous Christian authors as C. S. Lewis. Lewis caricatured Wells himself in his 1945 novel *The Hideous Strength*, where the character, Jules, is said to be a Cockney author out of date with science and with no comprehension of the foolishness he invokes. What did Wells really believe in the end? Was he such a logical being that he held no beliefs in spirituality? Or was there a glimmer of something more in his thoughts?

In his clever and philosophical book, *First and Last Things*, Wells gives us the answer:

> *"Now my most comprehensive belief about the external and the internal and myself is that they make one universe in which I and every part are ultimately important."* Page 133, *The Open Conspiracy and Other Writings*, H. G. Wells, London, Waterlow and Sons, 1933.

Wells argues that he is part of a "scheme", not that of a schemer, but of a wonderful intricate scheme of nature and that he is as important as anything else and so is a fly that drowns in a glass of milk. He does not know the scheme nor fully understands it, but stands in awe of its complexity, claiming that this makes him a "mystic" of the scheme. All, he says, is important and profoundly significant and if mankind would simply understand this, then he would have more respect, not just for one another, but for all of nature. This is H. G. Wells' "act of faith". He does not say that it is truth, indeed he openly states that it is his own personal working belief.

It is a merging of this belief in the scheme of nature and the injustice of the class structure that drives the works of Wells and is found within them. It is no different in this respect to the highly successful tales of Robin Hood, who is the spirit of nature fighting the injustice of the social class system. Is this why the tales are so successful and have such longevity? Is this why they speak to us all – because somewhere within us we recognize the truth of the tales?

Influence

H. G. Wells was a very clever man. He educated himself and rose above the lower middle-class ranks in which he was born and fought for their cause much of his life. He was a feminist in as much as he believed ardently in equality and he detested injustice. He was not afraid to change his mind publicly, which in my opinion is the mark of a truly confident man.

He gained wisdom from knowledge, from learning about

the sciences, history and the philosophers and indeed invoked them when he said that we teach our children about the philosopher and fail to teach them the philosophy. He hoped for a brighter future for mankind and yet predicted one of 'More of the same.'

Both in factual books and fiction, Wells attempted to influence society in the only way he knew, through his own creativity and writing skills. He succeeded to influence the world, but probably not always in the way he had hoped. His skill at foreseeing the future has given him the title, shared with Jules Verne, as father of science fiction and this influence has spread widely, opening up a whole new genre. I would suggest that the majority of people watching *The Time Machine* miss the real reason and message behind it and this can often be the case of messages portrayed in fiction. It is true as some would say that subliminally the message sinks in and it is also true that his other works of fact and philosophy are not so widely known or read. And so, maybe his social oriented messages and warnings within his novels didn't necessarily hit a critical mass and invade the consciousness of mankind, but maybe Wells did find another way of influencing society? Maybe he did have other means than writing…?

Many conspiracy theorists have presumed that Wells was a Freemason because many of his predictions have come to pass. They cite his assurance in *Anticipation: Of the Reaction of Mechanical and Scientific Progress upon Human Life and Thought,* that there would be a common currency in Europe (the Euro) and that he predicted a new world order, a statement many world leaders have since stated is required for world peace. They also point out that he uses the secret handshakes of Freemasons in his book, *The Inexperienced Ghost,* connected, says Wells with "a certain esoteric Masonry."

His book, *The Open Conspiracy* (1928), deals directly with the processes of everybody becoming involved in the formation of a new republic for the world, calling it an "outspoken secret society" and "open Freemasonry", which of course mirrors Wells' own opinions that religion and royal rule should be a thing of the past.

> "In all sorts of ways they will be influencing and controlling the apparatus of the ostensible governments." *The Open Conspiracy,* H. G. Wells, 1928, London.

The leaders of this new republic, according to Wells, have the moral responsibility to take action against the weakest elements, even if that may mean calling in the help of death. This, he calls, the ethical system, following natural rules, where the strongest survives and the weakest dies. These strongest individuals will of course not follow any ancient and out of date system such as religion, but be scientists, dealing with that which can be proven and which aids the future development and evolution of the humanity. These men of the New Republic will not be squeamish in facing and inflicting death and like Abraham, they will have the faith to kill.

His vision of this brave new world was the USA as the main central mass with the aid of a union of European States. In this way, conspiracy theorists back their claim that Wells was in fact not just predicting the future, but engineering it.

Of course, not all of his predictions came to fruition and we don't often hear of these. In the *Days of the Comet* (1906) Wells actually altered human nature by using a personality-improving gas that was shed by a comet's tail. This may not have come true and may be scientifically implausible (but not impossible) but it does show, yet again, his desire to change society for the better.

We have to remember that Wells was writing upon these subjects before the creation of the United Nations and yet he states that this new world republic must sustain a common fleet and protect, dominate and administer most if not all of the non-white states.

So, was Wells really so influential that he aided or engineered the manifestation of the United Nations? Did he really influence the creation of a European Union, a common currency, a world fleet and the belief that the white elite should police the world?

The list of friends and correspondences of H. G. Wells is immense and incredibly telling. From both Theodore and Franklin Roosevelt to Winston Churchill and Charlie Chaplin, the list also includes powerful media barons, influential writers and politicians, as well as top thinkers in the world such as Carl Jung, James Joyce, Thomas Hardy, Graham Greene and many more.

For many years Wells had been strong friends with the Huxley family. His biology tutor had been Thomas Henry Huxley, the grandfather of Aldous Huxley, a writer who was deeply interested in LSD and parapsychology. Sir Julian Huxley, with whom Wells and his son had collaborated on *The Science of Life* actually became the very first director general of UNESCO in 1945, bringing the strong evolutionary beliefs of Wells and Darwin to a powerful world stage.

It is easy to see that Wells' and Huxley's ideas of eugenics (death for the weakest) now had a new power base when we realize that Huxley in a speech given to the UN actually proposed it, stating that UNESCO must examine eugenics with the greatest care so that what may be currently unthinkable, becomes thinkable. (Julian Huxley, *UNESCO Its Purpose and Its Philosophy* (1946). Preparatory Commission of the United Nations Educational, Scientific and Cultural Organization.)

These beliefs in eugenics were not only shared by Wells but propagated by him. One of his string of lovers was Margaret Sanger, the founder of the organization known as Planned Parenthood and who wrote a book entitled *Pivot of Civilization* (1922). Wells actually wrote an introduction for the book in which he stated quite openly that mankind cannot make the perfect new world order and peace with ill-bred and ill-trained swarms of inferior citizens.

These are strong ideas and still quite shocking to a world that fought against a Nazi Party that held similar beliefs. And yet, his concepts of the new world order did in fact become reality and he was influential in their creation more than people may realize.

H. G. Wells on the Rights of Man was published in 1939 just as the Second World War was taking shape and was translated into 30 languages. It was highly influential in the minds of the popular masses and amongst politicians. Franklin D. Roosevelt, a friend of Wells, read the book and was highly influenced by it and indeed it may be conjectured that the hypothesis that the rights of man justified the war may have aided in the US joining the war. This was the idea that the war must be fought in order to enforce human rights over the nations with which you fought – even if this meant death and sacrifice. However what must emerge would be a new world order. Of course, Roosevelt used this same principle in 1942 when he declared that human justice and rights were the war aim.

Even many years before this in 1906 Wells had visited the United States and held high-level conversations with the likes of Theodore Roosevelt, when he had also taken a taxi cab and famously visited a local black brothel. In 1920, as we have seen, Wells traveled in the opposite direction and met with Lenin and Trotsky, being accused by Lenin of being 'a philistine'. Whilst here he bedded the married Moura Benckendorff, the aid and even lover of the infamous writer Maxim Gorky. Wells' sexual appetite seemed to match his political one.

Recent articles in the alternative thinking journal 'Fortean Times suggests

An indication of the influential power of Wells can even be found in one particular sexually oriented episode when one of his lovers slit her wrists and was rushed to hospital. She survived, but Wells pulled on his "friends" the media barons, Lord Beaverbrook and Lord Rothermere, to keep the story out of the press. (See http://www.ansible.co.uk/writing/ft-wells.html & http://www.forteantimes.com/features/profiles/122/hg_wells.html)

In 1940 Wells released his book, *The New World Order* and he called for the intellectuals of the world to help create the world government required for a peaceful world.

The name "United Nations" was devised by United States President Franklin D. Roosevelt and was first used in the "Declaration by United Nations" of 1st. January 1942.

Regardless of what we might think about H. G. Wells' political beliefs and sexual liaisons, whether we agree with his spiritual ideas and concepts of eugenics, the fact remains that he came from a poor background and made it to the top of his field. He may have failed to gain a seat in Parliament, which he did attempt in 1922 and 1923, but he somehow managed to influence the minds of the most powerful men on the planet. More than this, he influenced the literary world to such an extent that thousands of novels and hundreds of films and television adaptations are the result. There probably isn't a man or woman on the planet who has not in some way come into contact with the influence of H. G. Wells and that is the legacy of the man.

'The Open Conspiracy is the awakening of mankind from a nightmare, an infantile nightmare, of the struggle for existence and the inevitability of war. The light of day thrusts between our eyelids, and the multitudinous sounds of morning clamour in our ears. A time will come when men will sit with history before them or with some old newspaper before them and ask incredulously, "Was there ever such a world?" ' *The Open Conspiracy and Other Writings*, page 93, H. G. Wells, 1933, London.

Chapter 4

Jules Verne and the Power of Imagination

H. G. Wells is not the only man to have been called the father of science fiction. There was one who came just before and with whom he had some slight disagreement. His name was Jules Verne and he was a man who had a powerful imagination, albeit tied to the dogma of science, but not the religion of socialism.

For decades the tales of Jules Verne have inspired the imaginations of millions. Whether from books or films, cartoons or computer games, the stories of adventure and scientific fiction have seeped into the culture of the globe.

20,000 Leagues Under the Sea, *Journey to the Centre of the Earth*, *From the Earth to the Moon* and *Around the World in 80 Days* are just a few of the *Extraordinary Journeys* that Jules Verne immersed us in. Captain Nemo, the Nautilus and Phileas Fogg are household names.

The stories have changed, sometimes from manuscript to published novel, but more so as they became motion pictures. Projectiles became rockets, ships and trains turned into balloons and fiction with some science became science fiction.

Almost immediately biographers and critics began to analyse the writings and the man behind them. Some have claimed that his novels contained a pseudo-sexual message and others that he points us towards a hidden treasure buried by the infamous Knights Templar. To a great many more Verne was the father of science fiction and others claim he simply stole ideas and reformulated them.

But what is the truth? Was Jules Verne trying to relay a message? Or were his books just simple fiction for children? Was Verne a masterful genius or a storyteller with an overactive imagination?

His wife said that a secret burned at the heart of Jules Verne and that it almost crippled him. What was this secret?

This work investigates the man himself and those that surrounded him in order to discover the truth. We look closely at his most famous *Extraordinary Journeys* to try and discover the key to unlock the mysteries of Jules Verne. What we discover opens up a world of ancient secrets like never before.

Jules Verne

Jules Gabriel Verne was born on the 8th February,1828 into a France that was in almost constant turmoil. Revolution, republic, restoration of the monarchy, Empire and revolution again seemed to be the political world in which young Jules was fostered.

He was raised in the busy port of Nantes, where he spent a childhood of wealth, fun and exploration as the eldest of five children. Here, it was as if the political battles of Paris were a million miles away.

His mother was Sophie. She had no profession, but was happy, kind and incredibly imaginative. Always loving and affectionate, Jules Verne would hold her dear to his heart and, in his youth, he wrote beautiful poetry in her honour.

His father, Pierre Verne was an attorney and Jules was expected to follow in his fathers footsteps and to one day take over the family business.

Pierre was also highly religious and his spiritual fervour often led him to self-mortification, fasting and physical self-punishment. According to Jules Verne's grandson, Pierre would self-flagellate using the infamous scourge – a kind of

A French literary giant.

whip with multiple thongs. This simply had to affect the young Jules. In fact Jules Verne himself would suffer at the hands of his father with beatings and starvation's and this would also deeply embed itself in his mind. It is possible that the timid nature of Jules Verne in later life may have been a result of these times.

However, for many biographers it was in Nantes and the family's summer retreat on the Loire River, that the young Jules Verne fell in love with travel. He quickly learned about navigation and spent many hours messing around in boats, almost in an attempt to somehow escape the often harrowing home life.

He and his brother, Paul, were sent to St. Stanislas school where they heard tales of far-off lands from the boys that hailed from the Caribbean and New Orleans. Added to these were those of his sea-faring Uncle Prudent who often gave the children wonderful stories of South America and his exotic adventures. In comparison to their father, Uncle Prudent with his pirate past and seemingly ancient figure of authority must have been a blessing.

Later at St. Donatien College in Nantes, Jules Verne would study Latin and begin his begrudging journey to become a lawyer like his father. But his mind is already wandering at this stage and he writes "magical invocations in verse" which he stated later would never find their way into the public domain. This definite break from his father's religious zeal is an indication of just how early the young Jules Verne was seeking new and more exciting answers to the spiritual life.

Jules Verne dreamed of sailing away and high adventure, but the strong control of his parents, Pierre and Sophie, would land-lock the boy but not his mind. He wrote in poetry and prose of almost everything he observed and imagined and eagerly sought out exotic influences.

At home, when the stars were out, Jules and Paul would ask their father to reveal to them the faraway worlds with his telescope and they even imagined that one day they would be able to travel to them. Such was the period in which they lived, a progressive, forward thinking period of such possibilities that the only boundary was the imagination, and Jules Verne's was already at full tilt.

'Of all the books of my childhood, the one I loved the most

was Swiss Family Robinson. How many years I spent on their island! How passionately I joined in their discoveries! How jealous I was of their destiny.' *Jules Verne: The Definitive Biography,* William Butcher, Thunders Mouth Press, New York, 2006.

By the age of twelve, Jules Verne saw the sea for the first time calling himself the "ambitious Robinson."

It was also at this time that Verne entered his very first secret society, the *Nonboarders Club,* which included several future Freemasons and Rosicrucians, including the long-term friend Aristide Hignard. Many of these early friends would remain so for decades and they would often work together in various ways. Indeed it was with Hignard that Verne would make one of his most memorable of journeys, to Scotland and the land that held a deep fascination for him.

For Jules Verne, his Celtic heritage and family links to medieval Scottish archers was all he needed to find some legendary connection to more exciting times. He alluded to a noble past and had an air of Breton mystical tradition that suited him well and was fostered by the imaginative input of his mother, Sophie.

Now a young man, Verne moved to Paris where he studied law, being introduced to various literary circles and entering the world of the arts, much to his father's disdain. One strong point that we must remember from this period is quite simple: most literary circles at the time were highly influenced and almost overrun by various secret societies. These included the Freemasons, Rosicrucians and the Golden Dawn not to mention the possibility that the 18th century Bavarian Illuminati had already found a good foothold.

We need not assume these links however, for they are very open. Such writers as Alexandre Dumas and Victor Hugo were Freemasons and both were members of the same literary circles as Jules Verne and indeed were his personal friends.

Another highly influential character for the young Verne and a crucial key for deciphering him was the great American Gnostic, Edgar Allan Poe. In 1854, the works of Poe were translated for the first time into French and Jules Verne absorbed them eagerly, writing his very first science fiction novel, *A Voyage in a Balloon,* under Poe's influence.

Why is Poe so important in understanding Verne's work?

Well, not least because Poe was pioneering the modern science fiction writing, not just because of his incredible work in codes and ciphers within the novel, but also because of the spiritual and Gnostic influence he cleverly encoded in his works.

The Gnostic influence upon Poe and from Poe has been widely stated, but for us to have the eyes to see this influence within the works of Jules Verne, we need to have just a small knowledge of it's meaning and why it had to be hidden.

The concepts that Poe adhered to and indeed that fall beneath the surface of the world of secret societies is one of dualism. The soul, the true self, is trapped beneath a world of materiality and one must embark upon a sacred journey in order to find and retrieve this element, known as the divine within.

For millennia fables and folktales have hidden this basic psychological truth beneath symbolism – as if coding the ultimate treasure that all men search for. To 'Know thyself' is easier said than done and one needs knowledge or Gnosis, in order to overcome the many trials and tribulations that will befall all those who embark upon the quest.

In symbolic language we must die in order to be reborn. We must kill the person we have become to find the person we truly are. This is the death and rebirth element found within the Freemasons, the Rosicrucians and numerous other supposedly secret societies. For centuries these teachings were heretical to the Church and so all manner of methods were employed to hide them in plain sight. Alchemy, as we have seen with Paracelsus, was one such method and this kept alive the sacred teachings for several hundred years within the very Church itself.

Even in the time of Jules Verne such teachings were viewed as heretical and Pierre Verne would certainly have disliked his own son's involvement in this world. The notorious Freemason, Eliphas Levi, wrote extensively on similar matters in France during the time of Verne and was imprisoned for doing so. Jules Verne included this symbolism within his work and this is why we find a constant repetition of the circular journey and the numerology of 13, a symbol of death. Before moving on, we would do well to remember, that Poe's God, was the God of the abyss.

In spite of the diversions upon Jules Verne during this time he still managed to pass his law degree, but he knew from the very start that his destiny lay in other directions. He wrote plays, operatic librettos and many short stories and drew the consternation of his father who withdrew his funding.

For a time and with the help of his wise mother, Sophie, he supported himself as a kind of stockbroker whilst continuing to meet in literary circles, gaining the aid and guidance of Dumas and Hugo. As if to offset his financial worries he sought about for a wife and following several near-misses he settled on Honorine de Viane Morel, a widow with two children and a good income. Together they had a son, Michel, who was to disappoint Jules and the distance between them grew and grew.

Nevertheless Honorine encouraged his writing at first and from 1857 onwards he actively searched for a publisher, failing again and again to draw their patronage. It was then he met with the man he would later call his spiritual guide, Pierre-Jules Hetzel.

Hetzel was one of France's most important publishers, producing the work of Victor Hugo and the Freemason George Sand amongst others. He saw something in Verne and a lifelong partnership was formed. From this moment on Jules Verne found fame and fortune and latterly and quite incorrectly the title of father of science fiction.

The truth is that Jules Verne was not the father of science fiction. In fact his novels barely resemble anything of the sort. If volcanoes, the hollow earth, sails and big canons are science fiction then so be it. However, he even distanced himself from the emerging genre, stating that his own work was based in real knowledge unlike that of the new H. G. Wells whose imagination knew no boundaries of real scientific knowledge. Neither was Verne attempting some grand socialist statement, instead he was re-creating an ancient pattern of self-discovery.

He left the stockbroker business behind and threw himself into writing and playing the literary game with his new found friend Hetzel. In 1863 *Five Weeks in a Balloon* was published and two or more volumes were subsequently published each year thereafter.

His writing and stage-plays were now so successful that he had sufficient funds to buy a ship, the *Saint Michel*, which was replaced twice with even better vessels. In 1870 he was appointed as Knight of the Legion of Honour and to this day he remains the most widely read novelist in the world. His end was not so good.

By 1886 his mind was not so positive and his relationship with Hetzel seemed strained. Then on 9th March of that same year as he arrived home, his favourite nephew, Gaston, pulled a gun and shot him.

The bullet entered his left leg, causing him pain and torment for the rest of his days. The next day the papers were full of the story, but then something strange happened. Abruptly the stories stopped, Gaston was whisked away to an insane asylum, never to be seen again and the whole affair was hushed up. Nobody could discuss the event.

Eight days later Hetzel died and within the year Sophie, Jules Verne's mother, was dead. Verne fell into a sombre attitude of mind, as if he had lost everything that was dear to him. His kind and imaginative mother, who had supported him in his search for individuality from his religiously intolerant father was gone. His spiritual guide and replacement father, Hetzel was no longer there for him and his favourite nephew and replacement son had shot him at point blank range.

His world was falling apart, the psychological scaffolding that supported his very weakest parts had collapsed like a pack of cards. Death had already played a large part in the novels of Jules Verne and it is time now to turn to the message locked away within these incredible works.

The Works

Jules Verne's wife, Honorine said that something burned at the heart of her husband, a secret that he could not openly share and which at times appeared to suffocate him. These secrets are those of the treasure hunters, the seekers after wisdom and the world of the Secret Societies.

Jules Verne was a storyteller who fell in love with the world of adventure and literature and wanted nothing more than to tell his tales. Once initiated into the world of the literary circles, Freemasons, Rosicrucians and various others, he was entrusted with knowledge not meant for all mankind or as some would have it, the profane. This was knowledge that can and has been traced back to the times of the great Egyptian empire. The Freemasons and of course, the Rosicrucians both claim descent from these ancient times. In the rituals of the

Rubeae et Aureae Crucis from the early 20th century we find:

> "Know that the Order of the Rose and Cross has existed from time immemorial, and that its mystic rites were practised and its wisdom taught in Egypt, Eleusis, Samothrace, Persia, Chaldea, India, and in far more ancient lands, and thus handed down to posterity the Secret Wisdom of the Ancient Ages. Many were its Temples, and among many nations were they established, though in process of time some lost the purity of their primal knowledge." *Rubeae et Aureae Crucis,* no publisher stated.

This knowledge or Secret Wisdom of the Ancient Ages, revealed the divine or God in his works but not the Christ of any Christian denomination. No mention of Christ appears, but the Grand Architect of Freemasonry does. It revealed an initiation into the ancient mysteries, but not the rite of passage from the Holy Church. The world of Jules Verne is one of the occult, hidden from the eye, whilst all the time in plain sight.

One way or another, Jules Verne would tell his tale, even if forbidden by the laws of those who passed on knowledge to him.

In real life, he could not say a word and this is why he destroyed letters, unpublished manuscripts, accounts and personal papers before he died. It was the law of the societies from where he had derived his knowledge.

His novels were fiction and he cleverly coded his own Gnosis into them like a treasure map for those with the eyes to see. Not only was he aware of the heretical content that made him hide the knowledge from the Church, but he also needed to hide the fact from his masters.

According to several biographers, Jules Verne was hiding homosexual content in his novels and on a perfectly Freudian level we can understand why this would seem so. But it is plain wrong. One biographer states that the fact there is a complete absence for the desire of women in his *Extraordinary Journeys,* means that Jules Verne had no desire for women. This is missing the entire point and negating the facts that Verne married and bragged about visiting many brothels in his youth.

Extraordinary Journeys is the journeyman tale repeated again and again, and what is the journeyman? It is the tale of the path of the Freemason – a male society, a society of brotherhood. In this explanation alone, we have something the proponents of Verne's homosexuality do not – evidence! All those influences that surrounded Verne were from Freemasonic brotherhoods, even his so-called homosexual partner, Hignard, who travelled, lived and wrote with Verne, was a Freemason.

Brotherhood and the androgynous character are part and parcel of secret, occult and gnostic work. The influence of somebody like Edgar Allan Poe and the Gnostic secrets are in fact rife in all Verne's *Extraordinary Journeys* and even in the work from his youth which included the witch Abraxia. This is a wordplay on the Abraxus, which is a Gnostic god who reveals wisdom.

In truth, if Poe was the American Gnostic as many have claimed, then Verne was the French version.

We have already seen how Poe and Verne were interested and utilised codes and cryptograms within their work and in Verne's work these appear right from the start and begin the hero on his journey.

The novels begin with a fortuitous discovery of a clue or message, which needs deciphering. The discovery of the true treasure will only be revealed once the hero has solved the puzzle, which very often takes the whole novel to do. In fact, the clue is not just in the original puzzle, but is laid out before us in the entire work. This is a Freemasonic method and Verne hinted at this in his book, *In Search of the Castaways* when he explained that Masonic Lodges were signs of civilisation.

While humanity is taking a material path in *20,000 Leagues Under the Sea* or indeed almost any of the other works, our hero is sent on a quest to discover something else, something which lies beyond materiality. Captain Nemo has left the world of man behind and in his own words, he is dead. He is, in fact, dead to the material and exists beneath the waves, under the current of the times in the otherworld of the spirit and mind. Phileas Fogg argues with the members of the Reform Club, the social elite of a material world, that they are wrong and that his journey will prove it. Captain Hatteras in *The Adventures of Captain Hatteras* wanders the world of man, taking no part in it.

In probably the most famous of Jules Verne's novels, *Journey to the Centre of the Earth,* we have the prime example of the holistic Freemason and gnostic approach taken by Verne in his fairy tale retelling. Quite apart from the fact that he invokes the Mason's Grand Architect in the book we also have mention of the square and compass, the plumb line and the coded "true snails" which in French means Masons.

Journey to the Centre of the Earth is the path of the initiate. It is the trail, which leads to the discovery of the self and here Verne uses incredible alchemical symbolism on every level.

The story goes that Professor Lidenbrock and his nephew Axel must travel across Iceland, and then down through an extinct crater toward a sunless sea. This is the primordial water, the invisible gateway or barrier of the mind, from consciousness to the unconscious. Only by passing these waters will we find the true original self and in this story this is represented as the origins of mankind.

This is a psychological journey of battles to overcome and darkness to see into. Discovering the true self is often like this, we don't know what we shall discover and sometimes we lose our way, but we must continue the journey nevertheless. It is no different to the initiate entering the Temple or Lodge in darkness, undergoing trials and tribulations, making various sacrifices before the ultimate one of all. Here he must die to himself and be reborn, just as our heroes of *Journey to the Centre of the Earth* are reborn like the phoenix from the fiery volcano.

Lidenbrock refuses to give up his journey, stating that he

Is this Verne's most telling of tales?

will make it to the centre or die. In truth, the greatest of all Masonic symbols is the dot in the centre of the circle - the place of peace, the place where the true self resides. It is the perfect symbol, reflecting the Hermetic axiom, that which is above is like that which is below. The particle in the centre of the atom reflects the true source of energy and empowerment and our connection to this natural world is to find our true particle in the centre of existence itself.

The journey to the centre, to our very soul, must be in balance. We must remain upright at all times and the symbolism of the secret societies, the Gnostics and alchemy all show this. It would figure then that Jules Verne ought to point this very important element out in his work - and he does.

Professor Lidenbrock takes his young apprentice with him on his journey, Axel, his nephew. Is this an indication that Verne was the guide for his own nephew Gaston whom he loved as his own true son? Either way, the word Axel is indicative of balance and uprightness and the two must trudge to the very pole of the earth before they can begin their journey. They must raise themselves up in balance before they can descend into the darkest elements of the mind. It is the tale of the initiation, the journey of master and apprentice. Why does Axel go in the first place? It is because he has listened to his feminine principle, his voice of wisdom. His fiancé insists he go for 'When you return, Axel, you will be a man.'

The journey is again repeated in *From the Earth to the Moon*, when a bet is placed to see if man can reach the moon in a projectile when fired from a canon. In all the works of the alchemist one must begin with the Stone of the Philosopher's and the Canon or crucible is placed firmly upon Stone's Hill in Florida.

In the follow up book we discover that the projectile is forced into lunar orbit and falls into darkness and shadow. This is part of the initiatory process within the mind. And Verne compares the projectile to Mahomet's Tomb, which legend stated existed between heaven and earth, somewhere he says he would rather not be.

We also have a strange episode where the dogs on board raise a terrible noise as if coming to life. The female is given the name of the Goddess Diana and Barbican asks where Adam is to this Eve, so that new life can begin. A peculiar rambling about offerings to the Egyptian God Anubis and how the

An ancient journey set in the future?

dog should be cast in bronze by the king of hell – Lucifer, all revolve around the ancient mysteries revered by Freemasonry. The Dog king Anubis was responsible for resurrecting the great Green God himself, Osiris – and Osiris is in Freemason tradition, Lucifer himself.

Eventually they emerge into the light once again and following being trapped in the area of space known as the dead zone they find the strength within to return to earth like a bright falling star, baptised in the waters of the salty sea.

Alchemy is hidden in the texts and using a standard literary technique known as quaternity principle, which implies that where there are three main characters a fourth and important character will be lurking, we actually discover that Arne Saknussemm appears, or at least his descendent. This person is a prime informant, bringing information and knowledge and who is in fact a famous, but fictional 16th century alchemist, like Paracelsus.

Other works also reveal a distinctly Masonic influence. In *Robur the Conqueror* there is a Masonic Temple and in *Castles in*

California Dubourg holds his set square, compass and plumb-line to his heart whilst calling upon God. The Freemason motto found upon the coat of arms of the United Grand Lodge of England reads, audi, vide, tace, and means hear, see and be silent. It is the exact opposite of the description of Aristobulus from the *Green Ray* who is said to not listen, see nothing and never be quiet. In *The Underground City* Harry Ford is called the "solid journeyman" and an "apprentice" both terms used for Freemasons and indeed Harry was the son of a Mason.

There are strange but constant references to salt, salt lakes and salt rocks throughout Vernes work. There is good reason. It is the Freemasons role to create a new man and a new world. Salt is one of the three main elements from which the world will be built, for it is derived from the alchemical concept that salt is the unifier, the element of wisdom and science. It was more valuable than gold for many centuries and indeed, without it we would die.

Closely associated with the Freemasons are the Rosicrucians, a society sharing brothers with the Masons and finding origin back in the 17th century. They hold to similar degrees and secrets and are at heart full of Gnostic teachings. No wonder then that France, at the time of Jules Verne was a centre of Rosicrucian teaching and that much of this found its way into the work of Verne himself. Indeed, we may never know if Verne was a member of the Rosicrucians as Dr. Wynn Westcott, the Supreme Magus of the English Rosicrucian order himself said:

> "The revived Rosicrucian Lodges of the Continent of Europe are carried on with great privacy, and their members do not openly confess to their admission and membership." (1916, Rosicrucian pamphlet entitled *Data of the History of the Rosicrucians*, printed by John. M. Watkins - now the shop *Watkins* in London).

The Rose and the Cross or Rosicrucian appears in *From the Earth to the Moon, Travel Scholarships* and of course, the infamous *Around the World in 80 Days.* The hero is in fact the Master who rejects the material world and yet is master of it. Phileas Fogg is a member of the Reform Club, bearing the initials written by Rosicrucians, RC. He is a member of a brotherhood who must present themselves on the appointed day to their brothers, just as the Rosicrucian must. He is mysterious, holds great knowledge and has second sight.

Very similar concepts occur in *Robur the Conqueror* and *Master of the World* where Verne points out that the path to truth can only be found by one's own efforts and that we must follow the guide that is found within each of us. These were not just Rosicrucian sentiments, Verne used the exact same words.

We are told that materialism will be washed away before the new day can come. The language used is almost that of the alchemist with a great fire consuming all earthly matter, followed by a calm dawn and the revelation of treasure. This is not a literal treasure hunt, this is the Gnostic search for the true self yet again, the burning away of the material desires to discover a more beautiful truth within.

The name of this great hero, Robur, originally derives from the word for Oak. It is the symbol of strength used by many cultures and societies and is used extensively by the Freemasons, among them the famous Wood Cutters or Carbonari. These were a branch of the Freemasons also known as Wood Splitters. The term comes from the Gnostic Gospel of Thomas where Jesus says, 'Split a piece of wood, and I am there.' It is a reference to discovering the true self, the divine within.

The Wood Splitters were also known as the coal burners, hence Carbonari, because the fire would reveal the true flame or light of the wood. In *Around the World in 80 Days*, Passepartout is the second aid that Fogg had employed, the

A man at the height of his career.

The amazing tale that fascinated the world in fact holds a deeper secret.

first one being called the Forester. He is said to be 'a fine lad, who had, concerning his master, the faith of the coal burner.' Passepartout in French slang means nightingale, which is a bird that longs to see heaven, singing at the approach of a new dawn. Passepartout also means skeleton key, because he is the key to unlock the mysteries of the soul.

Phileas Fogg is therefore the master of wood splitters or coal burners and his very name, Fogg is an indication of the clouded mysteries he holds. He guides the nightingale towards the new dawn.

Phileas Fogg is the overall lover of fog and mist, cloud and fog were often used as terms within secret societies to advise the reader that there was a mystery afoot waiting to be uncovered. His very traits are those of the perfect Freemason or Rosicrucian, gifted with second sight, travelling the world in spirit, not lavish and giving money for noble causes anonymously. He is the perfect journeyman.

The God of the Freemasons and others is often termed the God of the Abyss – the divinity lost in the darkness of the mind which is truly the light. Christian fundamentalists have jumped on the great many references to Lucifer, the light bearer, who is this fallen angel and the very God of the Abyss himself.

Jules Verne virtually recreates Lucifer in Captain Nemo from *20,000 Leagues Under the Sea,* and he is often shown in mist and fog, diving into the depths of sea to gain not material goods, but knowledge and wisdom. Nemo himself says:

> "The sea is merely a supernatural prodigious existence... it is living infinity."

Nemo is an outcast of the material society, he is dead to the world, and even states that he is in fact dead. And yet, he lives beneath the waves, unknown and untouched by the world above. He is the shadow self of us all, full of knowledge, living forever in a sea of infinity, which is the mind connected to nature itself.

He finds Atlantis beneath the waves, a lost time and past of mankind. To the Rosicrucian, Atlantis was the spirit of nature or first matter, requiring alchemical fixation in order to be transformed. This simply means that the true self has to be discovered and made complete and firm before one can grow. Atlantis was said to be built in concentric circles, with the true king and queen ruling at the very centre. This is the place where one can really rule oneself.

His home, the Nautilus, is not a place of the Christian God for Verne states clearly there is no bread or wine. It is a place where this angel of light can peer into your very soul as Nemo does to our heroes. Verne calls the Nautilus the sacred ark, the carrier of the light of the divine.

So, who is this man Nemo? His name means no one, for he is everyone. "I have no name sir" he says. However we do find in *The Mysterious Island* that he is the son of an Indian

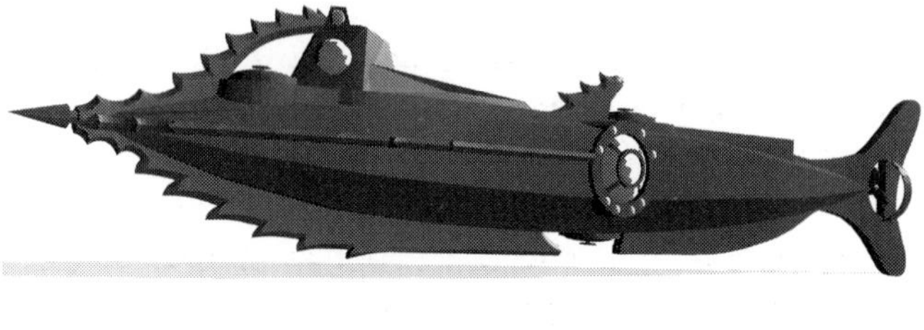

Probably the most famous submarine ever.

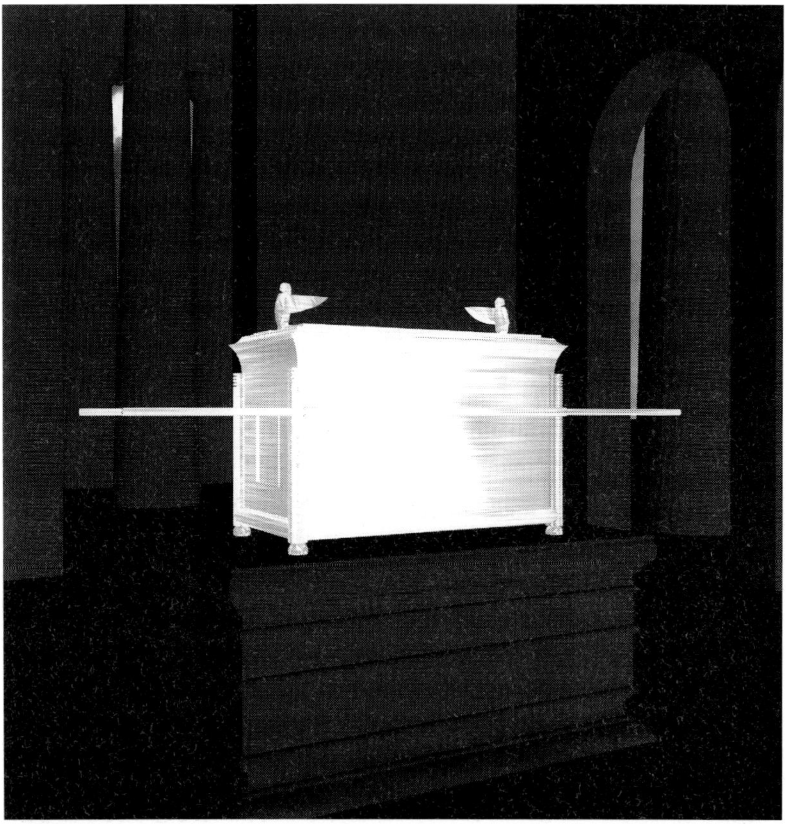

A sacred device and a sacred symbol for communicating with the divine, a symbol of Verne's own journey?

Rajah and his name is Prince Dakkar. This is what we learn in the book:

'From the age of ten years to that of thirty Prince Dakkar, endowed by Nature with her richest gifts of intellect, accumulated knowledge of every kind, and in science, literature, and art his researches were extensive and profound.'

Nemo is the all-round man of knowledge, but with the special ability of being closer to Nature than others. He is a true Shaman in many respects, a master of Gnosis or knowledge. We can see in this elements of the Rosicrucian nature philosophy, that by studying nature man could learn all knowledge and thereby aid society the better for it. It is no different to the concepts spoken of by Paracelsus – that understanding Nature means understanding ourselves and all things.

Does the name Dakkar have any meaning? It is another

word for the Tamarind Tree, which is the Tree of Knowledge from Indian lore, found at the very centre of the earth. He is the one connected to the Akashic Records, the place of all-knowing.

Like the Freemason or Rosicrucian, he travels the globe anonymously helping the oppressed with both goods and money. He is even said to have aided the Indian people in revolt against the British, a revolutionary implication very often applied to the Freemasons themselves.

In *Mysterious Island*, his final port of refuge, Verne makes a bold statement about mankind, that it is lost forever, because Nemo sinks to the ocean floor, locked away in his Nautilus coffin. As we have discovered, Verne calls the Nautilus the sacred ark and like the Ark it is lost forever, taking with it our connection to the divine knowledge. Thus, it is not the end, it is in fact the beginning in a paradoxical world of esoteric wisdom.

Nemo is no one, his numerology gives us the number 13, symbolic of death and of paramount importance to Freemasonry and other secret societies. Why should death be so important?

The truth is quite simple and it is the very death we should all seek. We must die to the old self, the self that grasps onto the material world. The ultimate symbol is death and for Nemo to have finally died in this way in the depths of the otherworld then he has truly risen in glory. As one of Verne's heroes, Barbicane, and hence Verne himself was to say:

> "If we die, the result of our journey will be magnificently enlarged. God himself will tell us his secret. In the next life, the soul will have no need of machines and engines. It will be identical with eternal wisdom."

Whether it is the road of the journeyman around the world in 80 days or the descent into the fires at the centre of the earth; whether it is the knowledge of one who has left the material world behind and living 20,000 leagues beneath the sea or the journey from the material earth to the celestial moon, the truth is that we are being taken along a very ancient path of psychological initiation.

Just because man has used his imagination over the centuries and clouded these simple truths in various forms of symbolism, societies and tales does not mean that we should no longer seek the truth. Jules Verne lived in a period that was emerging from religious constraint. There was literary and artistic excitement and Verne jumped aboard and went along for the ride. In fact he very often steered the course.

Behind the scenes there was a man who guided the way for Jules Verne from the very start and it is to this man that we now turn in-order to understand the *Extraordinary Journeys* a little better.

Hetzel

Pierre-Jules Hetzel was born in 1814 and died in 1886. He studied law in Strasbourg but by 1837 founded a publishing company that was to become one of the most powerful in France.

He was a well-known republican and in 1848 rose to chief of the cabinet in Foreign Affairs. However, following the coup d'Etat of the Second Empire he fled into self-imposed exile in Belgium, publishing clandestinely anti-government propaganda by such authors as Victor Hugo.

Following a softening and liberalisation of the political scene in France, Hetzel returned and set about publishing some of the most famous French artists and writers. His most

A troubled man in later years.

promising and most lucrative of course was Jules Verne himself.

Although Hetzel's name is not registered on any Freemasonic roles, this does not mean he wasn't a Freemason. The fact is that many lists were lost or destroyed, especially in the turmoil of the period and especially if your political and business adventures were not always in line with Freemasonry. The remaining facts however seem to show that Hetzel, if not a Mason, was certainly well-connected.

A great many of his authors such as George Sand, Victor Hugo and Alexandre Dumas were Freemasons and all of them friends of Jules Verne. Hetzel once said, concerning the kind brotherly love that Freemasons adhered to: 'There is no permanent love but that which has duty for its eldest brother, so that if one sleeps the other watches and honour is safe.' This is indeed the kind of very Masonic statement one would expect.

Hetzel was called by Jules Verne his spiritual father, a replacement of his own real father and for that of the church itself. Not only did Hetzel publish Verne, he censored him too and often to the point of incredible re-writes. The dark sombre endings of Verne are replaced with more positive and happy endings by Hetzel. The negative political statements are swiftly removed.

Hetzel stated openly that he wanted to publish morally worthy books, as if he were doing a service to the nation and so he amended Verne's work continually. Such characters as Captain Nemo were even changed from a vengeful Pole, seeking revenge over the Russian Czar to the character we know today. This, in fact, highlights a remarkable clue. It was Hetzel who re-made the rounded figure of our otherworldly deity, and not Verne. And so it was Hetzel who was the master to Verne, the apprentice, no wonder then that the Hetzel publishing empire was full to brim of members of secret brotherhoods.

This may now bring to light the reason that Verne never argued about the measly royalties and the blatant disregard Hetzel seemed to treat him with. The truth may be that there was more to the relationship than author and publisher.

Verne's novels, like any good fairy-tale or death-rebirth allegory are circular and it seems it was Hetzel who enforced this element in many of them – teaching the young Verne the rules of the game and bringing morally wholesome material for the masses whilst doing so. Like Ulysses, the tales of Jules Verne must return to their beginning, fulfilling the sacred code, the sacred journey back to oneself.

The Circle

And so in our analysis of Jules Verne, his writing and his friends we have come away with a glimmer of another world. This world is one of secret societies and occult knowledge often hidden from our eyes for a great many reasons.

One question remains unanswered. Why did Verne's replacement son, his nephew Gaston, shoot him on that fateful day in 1886? It is said that just before pulling the trigger, Gaston said to Jules Verne:

> 'You are being pursued. Someone wishes to kill you. There are people who have never forgiven you.'

Who were these people that pursued Jules Verne and why would a supposed assassin warn his target of such a thing? Why did Jules Verne destroy his papers, diaries and notes? Had he written more magical invocations as he had done in his youth? What secret was he hiding?

The evidence reveals that Verne was in a revolutionary

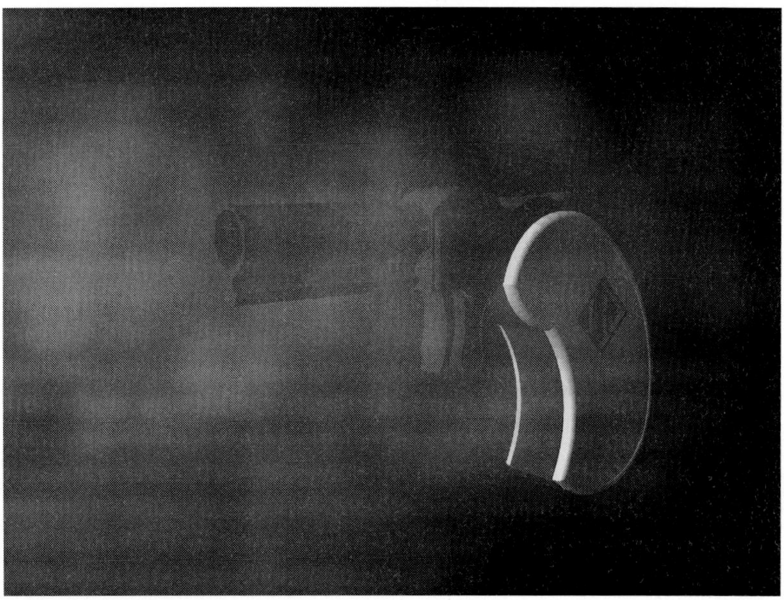

Why was Verne shot?

world of growing secret brotherhoods, which not only held sacred truths about ancient psychological methods, but were also creeping into vast positions of power. Government, religions, companies and literary groups were all overrun by Freemasons, Rosicrucians, Golden Dawn and Illuminati members and all were linked together with the thread of ancient Gnosis. Their aim to create an upright society of high moral standing, a new Jerusalem, or so we are told.

Was Gaston involved in this world of intrigue? Had he learned too much or was he the victim of a plot against Jules Verne himself? The question has to be asked, had Gaston somehow been got to? Was he under some drug induced control, able only to mutter those few words of warning?

Within days the whole issue had been entirely covered up and Gaston shipped off to an insane asylum never to be seen again. The newspapers were silenced abruptly and that kind of power can only be wielded by men of notable authority. A few days later the great Hetzel himself was dead and Verne would fall into a bleak state of mind, deepened by the death of his loving mother Sophie within the year.

His books now emitted a new darker element in the absence of Hetzel and political statements abounded. Suddenly the positive attitude towards mankind is missing from Verne's work and the almighty begins to issue vengeance. Humanity itself is threatened with extinction, as if Verne is offering us some kind of veiled warning against the religious and political leaders of the future.

Whatever the case, the truth may never be known, for all our evidence is gone, save for a few pieces of paper still held by the Verne estate under lock and key.

What we do have is a fascinating tale of the life of Jules Verne, often more fantastic than his own novels and certainly more of a puzzle. The overlying moral of the tale is clear, beware with whom you associate, for the circle of life is continual and what you sow, you may not wish to reap.

Conclusion

In March 1905 Jules Verne fell ill with diabetes. Slowly he fell towards the pit of death and was issued last rites on 23rd March, eventually dying on the 24th. The world's press announced the death and tributes came from far and wide, but none from any academic source. His family attended the funeral but nobody came from the Academy or government. His wife, Honorine burned the final papers and documents as requested and several years later the French managed to get enough money together to build a statue.

In a terrible storm a tree fell and took off the statue's head. It lay in the grass for a year.

Today, the name of Jules Verne is remembered and honoured by millions as the father of modern science fiction.

What was the secret that his wife said burned in his heart? Whatever the truth, his legacy is truly one of great storytelling and creative imagination matched with the genius of coded wordplay and hidden sacred and ancient truths. There is much yet to learn from the *Extraordinary Journeys of Jules Verne.*

Chapter 5

Bram Stoker – Beware of Invasion

H. G. Wells had a desire to change society; Paracelsus wanted to gain wisdom and insight; Jules Verne had a powerful imagination and understood the subtle esoteric world, and the secret cabals within the Knights of Malta fostered Eastern mysteries within their ranks. All these and more have seen or been involved in the power games of the world and the myths of ancient belief systems. One man who stood out, writing openly on the subject of the occult and with an incredibly popular creation of darkness, was Bram Stoker. His story relates closely to our themes. Gradually we have seen the concepts of Eastern mysteries creep into the West under the view of the Church, but none has spoken out against them. When I first decided to peer into the life of Bram Stoker, it was with a mind that he too might have had secret society links and ancient esoteric knowledge. I was surprised at what I was to discover.

> 'There are mysteries which men can only guess at, which age by age they may solve only in part.' *Dracula*, Bram Stoker.

What are the mysteries which men can only guess at? Have we finally solved all the puzzles?

Bram Stoker.

Dracula the book.

'To die, to be really dead, that would be glorious.' *Dracula*, Bram Stoker

Why would it be glorious to be really dead? What message was Bram Stoker trying to tell us in his tales of Dracula?

One of the darkest tales ever to emerge from the mind of man is the story of the arch-Vampire, Dracula. It took Bram Stoker seven years or more to unravel and re-tell the history and mystery of this ancient myth. In all this time, he must have uncovered more than just a simple horror story.

This work investigates Bram Stoker, his life, his friends, his associations and in so doing we find clues to the real truth behind the tale of Dracula.

We enter the dark world of the vampire, its past, present and future. We delve into the dark recesses within the mind of man and come away with mysteries only guessed at in each age. We discover that to be dead, really dead, is indeed glorious…

The Victorian Gothic World

In the middle 19th century, fashionable Victorian towns-folk were becoming bored with the monotonous classical style they saw around them. The Victorian age was one of solid tradition, but also of forward thinking and Great Britain saw itself as the main power broker on the world stage. A new style needed to be found, and one based firmly in strength and solid convention.

The Gothic style begun in the 12th century emitted a distinctly confident aura. The name itself is very telling and is based on the Goths who came from Sweden in around 150 AD. They had gained a reputation as a master-race, being excellent warriors and spreading far and wide. An example of this is found in the Spanish word for royalty, Gotos, which is derived from Goth.

But they also brought with them a peculiar Gothic Christianity, which seeped into the under-culture of the masses and mixed dark pagan gods with Christian saints.

By the Victorian age, the Gothic world was a distant and yet powerful past, with dark imagery of the night and the dream world. The change became known as the Gothic Revival and was aided by such writers as Sir Walter Scott and Lord Tennyson, who wrote gripping moralistic tales that spoke of an age when chivalry and power rested with the ruling and righteous elite. It was fantastic propaganda for the State and backed the revival of the Medieval style, whilst all the time retelling pagan stories in a new light.

Along with this style came a re-awakening in the literary guilds and arts societies. Not only had the Gothic Revival changed the landscape, it also pointed those men and women who had time to think, towards questions about the present contemporary world. Things were changing around them. The Empire was growing, but it was also vulnerable.

In the physical world, war was always just around the corner and battles forever being fought in one part of the Empire or another. But in the spiritual world, and the emotional mind of the people, another battle was being fought With every success abroad came a new threat, namely the influence of the newfound cultures upon the strict Christian West.

Misunderstood and misinterpreted, these new influences often took on a dark or sinister role in the mindset of the ordinary people and many writers utilised this element in their work. Despite being possibly misinformed, great authors, such as Sir Arthur Conan Doyle used these perceived threats within their work and some revealed a tendency towards racist bigotry that would not be tolerated today.

From the Christian perspective, there was indeed a darker element underpinning the invasive influence from abroad. Some even took up the cause of these invaders and aided them by translating revered texts and claiming some ancient and sacred truth lay at the heart, awaiting discovery.

A battle ensued in the public domain between newly formed societies on the one side, such as the Theosophists, and the established sciences on the other, which were still very much owned by the Church and State.

These influences from cultures such as the Hindu and Muslim world spread across the West once again, as they had during and after the Crusades. Yet again, followers or adherents were classified as occultists and demonised by the Church. However, the battle was not always in the open. Often artists and writers would hide their own beliefs under allegory and metaphor as if to avoid the demonising Church and the loss of sales. The true skill was in being able to successfully craft the esoteric secrets into a particular work, whilst still attracting a buying public.

In the years that followed, analysts such as Michel Lamy and William F. Friedman, (Edgar Allan Poe, Cryptographer, *On Poe: The Best from "American Literature"*. Durham, NC: Duke University Press, 1993. p. 40–41) studied the work of the greatest writers and discovered that there were indeed messages being passed on, subtly. Victor Hugo, Alexandre Dumas, Edgar Allan Poe, Jules Verne and many more are now believed to have hidden occult knowledge within their work.

The literary groups were overrun with Freemasonry and Rosicrucian tendencies, who themselves taught ancient wisdom as passed down from non-Christian sources. And yet on the surface the West was staunchly Christian, which most observers have agreed was a perfect device for controlling the

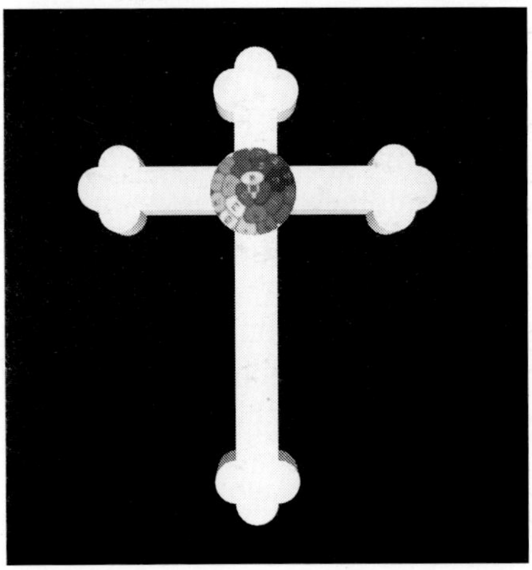

The yellow cross and Hermetic symbolism of the Rosicrucian Order.

growing masses. Freemasonry under Victoria's reign flourished to the point that it would have been embarrassing if one were not a member. By 1840, there were over 100 Lodges in London and 340 in the provinces. Weekly Freemasonic newspapers were sold, openly, in newsagents and its causes promoted by the Royalty, but only to those of the ruling elite and social upper classes. The brotherhood, fraternity and equality of the Freemasons had taken a turn, full circle back to the original power brokers, landowners and even the hierarchy of the Church and State.

On the one hand, the rulers needed to maintain strong control and discipline, and the Church gave this element in a mostly non-violent manner. But on the other hand, these same religious leaders, writers, artists, industrial giants, politicians and a whole host of others, were intrigued and beguiled by the world of mystery that was opening up before them.

Battle lines for the mind were being drawn and nobody had a map. A war was about to break out and precious few could decide which side to take. It was in this world that Bram Stoker emerged and it was of this world that Dracula was finally formulated.

Bram Stoker

Bram Stoker was born in 1847 in Dublin, Ireland, to Abraham Stoker and Charlotte Thornely. He was one of seven children and was baptised at St John the Baptist church where he regularly went.

He was bedridden with a mysterious illness, making a complete and unexplained recovery at the age of seven. This gave him time to think:

> "I was naturally thoughtful, and the leisure of long illness gave opportunity for many thoughts which were fruitful according to their kind in later years." http://en.wikipedia.org/wiki/Bram_Stoker

His mother told him tales of fairies and folklore and must have mentioned the Sidhe (pronounced Shee), a kind of fairy vampire. Did these early tales sink deeply into the mind of this young boy?

His recovery was swift, however, and by the time he reached Trinity College in Dublin he was actually excelling at physical activity, being a named University Athlete. Along with this came a keen interest in history and philosophy, joining the College Historical Society as auditor and becoming president of the University Philosophical Society. Indeed, his very first paper reveals a distinct understanding of what is required of the writer and was entitled *Sensationalism in Fiction and Society*.

By the late 1870's he was working as a civil servant in Dublin Castle and had written several theatre reviews, short stories and published a non-fiction work with the not very sensational title of *The Duties of Clerks of Petty Sessions in Ireland*.

But things were about to change and following a rave review by Stoker of *Hamlet* the imperious actor and star of the show, Henry Irving, invited him to become his manager at the Lyceum Theatre in London. The civil servant jumped at the chance and, in the meantime, in 1878 he married Florence Balcombe, who had previously been the suitor of Oscar Wilde.

Bram Stoker was to spend the rest of his life in the epicentre of the new Victorian world, London, and with the influence of Henry Irving he enjoyed the high society. In 1879, Florence and Bram Stoker had an only son whom they christened Irving Noel Thornely Stoker in honour of their newfound friend.

Gothic architecture example.

The new influences on Stoker must have been profound. One of these influences was Sir Arthur Conan Doyle, whose home Stoker called "a fairy pleasure house". Indeed, their mutual interest in the occult, fairies, plays and of course, Henry Irving, had drawn them together.

There was another element that may have drawn these various characters together. Almost all of the associations of Bram Stoker, including his own brother, were Freemasons.

Like the Gothic world, Freemasons claim to not be a religion and yet they hold dear to the Great Architect in the same way the Goths had held to their pagan Gaut or God. They were an influence for the esoteric, for the occult, and we find that many of the writers and artists, cult leaders and theosophists were members of the Freemasons. It was a hub of thought, intellectual discussion, brotherly assistance and above all, it offered a sense of belonging, just so long as you were rich, powerful or of value in some form.

And yet, the records show no mention of Bram Stoker as a Freemason. There was a lot of speculation both during Stoker's lifetime and following, that he was initiated in Dublin, but the Grand Lodge of Ireland has no record of the event.

It is also rumoured that he was a member of the occult group, the Golden Dawn[1] and even the Rosicrucians – both groups linked with Freemasonry. A fleeting glimmer of his understanding of Freemasonry is said to be found in *Dracula* and indeed many have stated that it is a Freemasonic work. In his book *The Lair of the White Worm* we find the phrase "We two are, I take it, tiled." This is a Freemasonic phrase.

Whatever the case, whether Stoker was a Freemason or not, the truth is that he was a man living in a world of prominent men who were almost all Freemasons. The influences upon him must have been substantial and the pressure to join with his fraternal brothers immense. In fact his own master, his employer, a man whom Stoker admired till the day he died, was a Freemason.

Bram Stoker died in 1912 and his ashes placed in Golders Green Crematorium in London. In 1914, his book *Dracula's Guest* was posthumously published by his widow.

Today, Bram Stoker is remembered as the father of *Dracula* and dozens of film adaptations, books and even computer games speak of his legacy. But did he cleverly encode a secret message into this timeless work of fiction?

The facts are simple. Bram Stoker was a clever, thoughtful man with a degree in Mathematics and even being invited to the Bar as a lawyer. He worked under a Freemason actor and had Freemason friends and relatives. He researched tirelessly the myths and folklore of the world and he lived in a time of Gothic and esoteric revival.

Did Bram Stoker plant elements from all these influences into his works that still hold a message for us today?

Dracula

Regardless of modern popular perceptions, Bram Stoker did not invent the vampire, nor did he create Dracula. Both these and other elements within his famous novel had appeared before, but he did link them together.

In his research, Stoker read such works as *Transylvania Superstitions* by Emily Gerard and met with Arminius Vambery the Balkan expert. He was influenced by Sheridan Le Fanu's *Carmilla,* an erotic tale about lesbian vampires and John Pollidori's *The Vampyre,* with a character based upon the seductive Lord Byron.

Stoker fused these stories together into a coherent and exciting tale that struck a chord with the masses. He finally had some use for the knowledge he had gained when he wrote his first University Paper, *Sensationalism in Fiction and Society.*

The story begins with the English solicitor, Jonathan Harker, visiting Count Dracula's castle in the Carpathian mountains on the border of Transylvania and Moldavia. The purpose of the mission is to provide legal aid for Dracula to buy real estate in England and thus bring his vampirism to Great Britain and the home of the teeming millions.

Harker quickly discovers that something is not quite right and that he is in fact prisoner of this strangely nocturnal Count. Then one night he falls under the spell of the three brides of Dracula and is only saved at the last minute by the Count himself, who needs Harker alive for his legal transactions. Eventually Harker manages to escape from the castle and flees back to England.

We next find that the Russian ship, *Demeter,* has run aground at Whitby with all the crew missing, except the captain who is found dead at the wheel.

Dracula in the form of a large dog is said to have leaped

The classic Dracula image.

ashore and pretty soon is menacing Harker's fiancée, Mina Murray and her friend Lucy Westenra. We are then introduced to three gentlemen, Arthur Holmwood, Quincy Morris and Dr John Seward, who each propose marriage to Lucy.

Soon, Lucy begins to waste away and her suitors begin to worry. Dr Seward calls on his old friend Abraham Van Helsing, who tries in vain to revive Lucy with blood transfusions. The Westenra household is then attacked by a terrifying wolf and Lucy succumbs to death.

She is buried soon afterwards, but quickly reports of a beautiful lady stalking children at night emerge and Van Helsing realises that Lucy has become a vampire. The three suitors and Van Helsing track her down and stake her heart, finishing her off with a beheading.

Now Jonathan Harker and Mina join forces with the team and track Dracula down, but the Count manages to get to Mina and bites her three times, feeding on her blood and creating a kind of spiritual bond between them.

Mina's mind wanders between the living world and that of the undead as the blood of the vampire surges through her veins. It seems the only way to overcome this cruel torment is to kill Dracula himself, who flees back to Transylvania.

The group follow in hot pursuit and before sunset, catch him, shear his throat and stab him with a Bowie knife. He slowly crumbles to dust before their eyes and Mina is freed from the spell.

This, in short, is the tale of Dracula. The question is, are there any clues to the real message that we can uncover?

The first and most obvious place to begin is with the main character himself, Dracula. Not surprisingly, there has been a lot of debate over the creation of Bram Stoker's Dracula and the possibility that the characters' origin lay with the infamous historic Romanian ruler, Vlad the Impaler.

Vlad the Third, Draculea of Wallachia, is a controversial 15th century figure. In Romania he is often heralded as a hero and elsewhere as a demon of the highest order. It is said he impaled his victims in their thousands but also that he was a good ruler. Whatever the case, his title, Draculea is derived from his father's title of Dracul, with Dracula being the son of Dracul.

Although the title took on the meaning of demon, in fact it means dragon, being derived from the Latin *Draco*. This shall become important, not least because the dragon was the winged serpent. The title, in fact, comes from Vlad the Second's membership of the Order of the Dragon begun in the early 15th century by the King of Hungary and Holy Roman Emperor, Sigismund. It is in fact originated in the Order of St. George from the 14th century, an inference to the dragon slaying, and hence, pagan slaying abilities of Christianity. Its main aim was to protect the West against the Ottoman Turks even though at the time various people described it as "a pagan rite".

The argument amongst fans of Dracula and Stoker is quite simple. One camp believes that Vlad the Third was the original Dracula and that Stoker used him in particular. The other camp states that there is no evidence for this. Let's take a look.

In the book, *Dracula*, Bram Stoker points out the very old European tradition that bad things occur on St. George's day unless one has spiritual protection. This tradition goes right back to pagan times, when this dragon slaying implied the death and destruction of the old ways by the Empire building Catholic Church. This itself links nicely with the Order of the Dragon of St. George of which Vlad was a member.

In addition to this we know that Bram Stoker befriended

The symbols of this famous Eastern Order.

Arminius Vambery the Balkans expert and read Gerard's *Transylvania Superstitions.* Originally, Stoker was to call his character Count Vampyr, but following his reading of Romanian folklore and history he changed his mind.

Dracula was from the Szekely's who are a distinct people from Central and Eastern Europe. They still hold to the symbol of the sun and moon of their ancient gods and this symbol reveals that element of being between two worlds – night and day.

It seems then that the name itself must have derived from these Transylvanian histories. This does not mean, however, that the traits of Dracula were copied from Vlad the Impaler. In fact, the traits of Dracula lie elsewhere and are not the result of one character in particular.

It shall become obvious as we uncover more of the subtle codes just what Dracula is supposed to represent. For instance, there is a clue in the very method used to deliver Count Dracula to the shores of England.

The ship, the Demeter, a Russian vessel, is used and all aboard die mysteriously. The first obvious point here is that Demeter is the Greek goddess and nourisher of youth. It is she who preserves the life and death cycle, being the giver and the taker. Here, in Stoker's book, she is the bringer of Dracula, the taker of life. The implication is simple, that Stoker is telling us some sacred truth is to be revealed, for Demeter is the protector of the sacred. All those profane aboard have died and this mother ship has given birth to the dark lord.

The ship is also Russian and there were plenty of reasons for Russia to be implicated as the deliverer of this invasion force, but we are told that this is a sacred ship, a mother goddess bringing some message. There was a motherly figure who was extremely famous in Stoker's day and who influenced his writings whether directly or indirectly. Great arguments surrounded this woman of infamy for her outspoken ways and her leadership of the cult of Theosophy. Her name was Madame Blavatsky and she was Russian.

It was Blavatsky who would influence not just Stoker, but hundreds of other artists, writers and all manner of people. Conan Doyle was one of these and of course, he was also a good friend of Bram Stoker.

What she offered was entry into the world unseen; she hinted at arcane and esoteric secrets hidden within the teachings of the East and, in fact, was an Eastern Star Freemason. Her world was the Otherworld and Dracula is quite blatantly of this otherworld, for he cannot cast a shadow, nor be seen in a mirror.

Simply put, Blavatksy and her Theosophical Society were blamed by a great many people in the Christian West for undermining their traditions, lifestyle and power base. In fact her rapid rise to fame and the growth of similar societies was a big worry indeed. Annie Besant, another prominent Theosophist and feminist, along with Blavatksy, were blamed

The lady at the head of the Eastern invasion force?

for the loss of India to the British Empire in later years due to the constant undermining of the traditional stance for supposedly humane reasons. Annie Besant was also a member of the Fabian Society (along with H. G. Wells,) a socialist reformer, as we have seen, and a threat to religious and royal rule.

How does this help our understanding of Bram Stoker's message? We know that Stoker chose the name Dracula and that he must have learned this from his studies on Romania and Vlad. We also know that the name Dracula means the son of the Dragon and was a title given to members of the Order of the Dragon. How does this relate to the Theosophists and the world of the occult?

Well, we also learned earlier that the dragon was in fact the winged serpent and the serpent has been worshipped across the world for millennia, long before Christianity stamped its authority over the serpent worshippers. The image of Archangel Michael and St. George killing the dragon, not to mention Mary crushing the serpent underfoot and a great many more, are images of the Christian Church overcoming the power of the pagan serpent worshippers. The druids were known as adders and almost every culture from Egypt to India held the serpent sacred. The question is why and what does this have to do with Dracula?

The Eastern traditions highlighted by Blavatksy and many others all revolve around the serpent – a creature that by this time had become demonic due to the Christian Church's attitude. This serpent was seen by many as a spiritual force within the human being – a kind of energy that needed tapping in order to self-realise and meet god. Of course this was utter blasphemy in the Christian West and the onslaught of these ideas upon the fabric of Victorian England was seen as an invasion of the darkest nature. A great many books both for and against this element of Eastern religions were published and battles raged in the press.

In addition to this, the ritualistic practices of those following the newly reformed serpent spirituality embarked upon misinterpreted elements of a sexual nature, mistaking divine union and the often crude symbols and carvings of the East as literal instructions. This could easily be the reason for Dracula's overt sexual serpentine energy spoken of by Bram Stoker.

Dracula is the human form of this otherworldly serpent-dragon beast, delivered to these shores by Demeter, the mother goddess from Russia. His intent was to come to the land of the teeming millions and to thereby repopulate the globe with the living dead. He is the symbol of the new wave of Eastern spirituality, an abhorrent sexuality and dark occult practices that so frightened the stuffy traditionalists of Christian Victorian England.

Almost everybody misinterpreted everybody else because of religion and belief. The Christians were set and safe in their trinity, the new age mystics adamant and yet fresh to millennia-old cultures and in between linguists struggled with interpreting complex words and changed the entire meaning. Spiritual rebirth very quickly became Gothic death.

In truth, it was the concept of the Eastern Maya which was misunderstood in the West as death, where, in fact, it is the concept of illusion which we must see through in order to realise the true state of existence. It is the true death that must be obtained, not the literal death, and this is why Dracula, the embodiment of the serpent deity says: "To die, to be really dead, that would be glorious." In the Eastern belief, he is searching for escape from the material world and it is a sacred journey, requiring sacred blood offerings.

This same esoteric notion is spoken and ritualised in many occult groups and societies, not least of which is Freemasonry. Here, the initiate must die to his old self in order to be reborn within the new family. It is the ritual of control and quite often blood itself must be drawn as a sacrifice, an offering and a sign of blood brotherhood.

Indeed, the blood ritual has been part and parcel of human tradition and religion for as long as the vampire itself.

The Vampire

The vampire has been part of the human subconscious for a very long time. In modern popular folklore the vampire is evil, with intent upon taking our very soul and sapping our life-blood in order to survive. These concepts are deeply rooted in the fear of the unconscious mind – the dark recesses of our very selves.

The word vam simply means or even "in preference to". The word pire means fire, and so a vampire is he who stands before or in preference to fire. This can sound very strange but we have to see it in relation to that small animal always associated with the Vampire – the bat. The evidence for this comes from Sir Walter Skeat's work, *English Etymology,* where Vampire is spelled Vampyre and is divided as vam and pyre. In this respect pyre is fire and vam derives from avant meaning before. Later texts on etymology work on the more modern spelling of Vampire and split the word into vamp and ire derived from the Serbian vampir/upir which itself is borrowed from a Turkic term (upyr) for witch. Nobody can agree on the exact etymology of the word, but it does include many meanings, such as "to fly", "fire", "before" and is found rooted in dozens of languages with most etymologists stating that it was derived from earlier Pagan beliefs.

Bat derives from the word bakke (Middle English (http://en.wiktionary.org/wiki/bakke#Middle_English)) or Nattabakka Old Swedish (Night Bat) and is in fact related to much more ancient concepts and means the land of light or fire or even "to watch" and "deep within" (Turkic). The sacred heart of Islam, Mecca, was once known as Bakka, because it holds the starry stones that fell from heaven – the light of the night sky falling to the ground and which are now kept in a perfectly black state like the night itself. Here we are finding that the bat was, in fact, not something of evil, but a carrier or transition device between the world of man and the world of the deities. It traversed the twilight, it overcame the fear we humans had of the night and therefore had preference to the light or fire.

This fire spoken of by our ancestors was a unique experience, an altered state of existence and attributed to the fiery serpent energy – the fire of the dragon, which can give you wings.

Because of the obvious pagan elements to these concepts and because it spoke of a method of meeting the divine without the need for the Church, the Catholic world erupted with propaganda and vengeance against all things bat-like. Pretty soon the vampire was a bloodthirsty tyrant, pulling upon the ancient blot or blood rituals as evidence.

Even the very bloodlines of those in old Europe were tainted and given false histories. The dragon or serpent worshipping past that pre-dated Christianity across Europe was sullied by naming Dracula, the arch-dragon himself, as the head of the vampire order. Evidence of this dragon-linked past comes through in many ways. For instance the Magyar people have a name for the highest initiation available to the Shaman, *Tethatu*, which translates as "one who talks with dragons."

In fact, these were remnants of a pre-Christian era that worshipped the serpent and utilised various methods of finding the fire within, including blood rituals and ecstatic states. This place of peace within ones own mind was known to the Hindu's as the void – a metaphysical concept not easily understood in the classical Christian sense.

In time, the word crept into western language as Vidya and eventually Wicca. This gave rise to the term we now have for those shamans of the past, witches. These were the ones who could access the otherworld on our behalf where images of bats and serpents abound.

The winged serpent or dragon is a universally accepted archetype, as is the bat. There are physical reasons and internal psychological reasons, they were creatures of both the physical night and the mental night.

These elements to the untrained and Christian mind would have been horrifying and this was the genius of Stoker – bringing the night out of our own minds to terrify us.

Other Clues

There are other clever devices utilised by Stoker in Dracula. For instance Abraham Van Helsing is the character who is brought in to save the West from this evil Eastern concept. In a sense Stoker is here offering himself up as the sacrifice in a paradoxical esoteric manner, for his own name is Abraham and Helsing is derived from the word "hals" meaning neck or throat. This is therefore the sacred offering of Abraham, through which God will bless the whole family or State.

But there is something much more enlightening about Van Helsing when we look into one of the main influences for this character – the German Professor, Max Muller.

Although Van Helsing is supposed to be Austrian in the book, he, in fact, speaks German and the original manuscript has him as such. Max Muller was German and a contemporary specialist in religion and mythology. These are the required sciences to battle the likes of the Theosophists, not medicine and mathematics and Max Muller did, in real life, take on Blavatksy herself. Indeed, Stoker himself wrote that

Helsing was to be "a German professor of history" named Max Windshoeffel, but these changed to Austrian professor and Van Helsing in order to distance the character from his real life counterpart.

It was Max Muller who first used the word "theosophy", later stolen by his arch-rivals the Theosophists. He said that Blavatsky had done much mischief in her lack of understanding the Hindu religion and argued against her so-called secret doctrine.

Bram Stoker knew Max Muller and of Blavatksy and he was aware of the famous battle of words that constantly surfaced in the press. It was claimed at the time that Stoker himself was a member of some magical society akin to the Theosophists or the Golden Dawn, but there is no evidence of this.

Instead it appears that Stoker is highlighting a very real fear amongst the Western Christian world – that these new cults were taking positions of power and invading the lands and the minds of the people.

Indeed, Stoker even used code to point this out with Dracula's first victim being Lucy Westenra. Westenra represents the West, as opposed to the mystical East and the name Lucy derives from light itself.

Dracula has therefore turned out the light of the West…

In another name we have yet more code. John Seward is the man who calls upon Van Helsing and his name reveals his true conduct. John is a name of solidity, a true old-fashioned name of one who can be trusted and meaning God is merciful. Seward, again is strong and means guardian of the sea. John Seward is the strong British man guarding the shores against invasion.

Another element practised widely by the occultists was trance-inducing hypnotism and we, not surprisingly, discover that Dracula is capable of this mysterious art, controlling the mind of the weak. But science too was developing hypnotism and it was becoming popular in Stoker's time. It is therefore fitting that Van Helsing also has the power of hypnotism, but not by any mysterious otherworldly method, but by pure scientific reasoning. The science of the West is here, overcoming the mystical occult world of the East.

In other works by Stoker there are similar battles between the good Christian West and the evil serpent. In *The Lair of the White Worm* we have the Lady Arabella, meaning prayerful, battling the serpent here called the worm, which in fact means serpent.

In the same book, Bram Stoker makes the point about the madness that inflicts those who stray into the world of this ancient serpent. Edgar Caswall is afflicted by the torment of madness, which is here depicted as egotism:

> "Come to me! You shall see now what you are despising, what you are warring against. All that you see is mine – the darkness as well as the light." *The Lair of the White Worm,* Bram Stoker, http://publicliterature.org/books/lair_of_the_white_worm/xaa.php

These are the words of the Gnostic God of the abyss – the lord of light and dark, the one who has power of the dual nature of the mind. At the very touch of his hand, Stoker claims, the power mounts up and up. It is the serpent energy, the sexual energy, spoken of by occultists for generations and demonised by the Church.

This serpent is the coiled one of Hinduism that must rise and fall like a wave and Stoker makes this very point saying that this serpent is coiled, it rises and falls and that no-one can see it, for it lies within each of us. Today modern science is unable to find this elusive serpent energy other than in the mind of the adherent. It appears that we are witnessing an age-old psychological trip, induced in various ways including sexual, meditative and the use of drugs. Chemical effects, and heightened brainwave functions, alter the state of mind of the individual to such a degree that he or she begins to be encased in emotions that are as old as the system. Jung called many of the experiences whilst in this state, archetypes – for they are universal and part of our nature. Even though in our modern era, scientists are breaking down the experience into distinct elements such as chemical and electrical, there are still major problems. We live in a world where enlightenment and escape from boredom are just as important for individuals and so they seek out these ancient forms. There may be no problem with that, except there are psychological problems that can often come with these experiences if not carefully approached in wisdom. Psychosis cannot only bring on trance states in individuals, but it can also result from them – so beware, Bram Stoker has already warned us of the devilish serpent energy.

It is the serpent from the Garden of Eden, although Stoker

calls it the Garden of Evil and our hero is none other than Adam. This first or prime man meets Lilla, who is really Lillith, the same Lillith whom Jewish myth states was wed with Adam. Lillith is the serpent deity herself and she tempts. However, Adam overcomes and marries Mimi – her name being another form of Mary, the mother of god.

The snake is seemingly of paramount importance as the adversary for Bram Stoker, in *The Lair of the White Worm*, *Snakes Pass* and *Dracula* the symbolic references abound. In *Dracula*, Harker's carriage is sent on a "serpentine way" in a manner like "the serpent" and even the peasant's cart has a long "snake-like vertebrae."

Bram Stoker was indeed pointing towards a serpentine mythological past and warning of the consequences that would befall the Christian West should the battle be lost. He implicated modern occultists and created a fictional battle of light against darkness. It is a tale as old as man, for the true light and dark resides within us and must be balanced and controlled in the same vein that Stoker points out.

Stoker's tales are not initiatory stories like those of Jules Verne, they are instead warnings against losing balance and succumbing to the dark forces that rage within each of us and within society in general. The seemingly solid traditional Christian values of Victorian England were under threat. Not from some invading army but within the spiritual dimension.

They will come in the night, for they reside within. They have no shadow for they are the shadow self. Their reflection cannot be seen for they do not reflect the light. Like black holes they suck the very life-blood from society. They are the serpent ones who must be crushed, impaled, beheaded – the serpent is a powerful force not to be toyed with. This is the message of Bram Stoker.

His employer, Sir Henry Irving, a Freemason and moralist was seen as an actor trying to revive a Gothic style in his productions. He produced plays which consistently fostered the sense of good and evil, right and wrong and his lead characters would do battle with personal demons in order to achieve a higher level of consciousness. In a distinctly esoteric statement he would often play both the role of the hero and the adversary, revealing that we are all both sides of this same coin.

Irving revived the supernatural medieval focus in the theatre, revealed the ancient battle within the mind of man himself and his younger employee would follow suit in print. Could Stoker have been Irving's young Freemasonic apprentice? We shall never know, but just like Jules Verne, the young writer seems to have been guided by an elder.

Conclusion

The whole tale of Dracula is quite circular. In reality, Bram Stoker was telling us the age-old story of the battle between the pagan East and the Christian West and between the controlling powers and the spiritual world. There is little difference between the world of Dracula invading the West and Order of the Dragon continuing the worship of the serpent-dragon beneath the very noses of the Church.

The Catholic Church believed many centuries ago that they had stamped out the last of the serpent worshippers and heralded their super heroes in St. George, St. Michael, St. Paul and St. Patrick – their serpent crushing warriors for Christ.

But Bram Stoker revealed to us that the battle was still afoot only a hundred years ago, and that the ancient concepts of trance-induced states often attributed to the serpent sexual energy, were still very much alive. This time, he warned, the dark influence was coming in legally, as Harker the hero of *Dracula* is employed by the Count to make his invasion legal.

Was it a warning or just a simple statement? Who's side was Bram Stoker on? Was he simply observing a cultural shift or was he trying to affect it? Whatever his wishes, he has created a cult following for the dark lord of Transylvania like never before and raised up the stakes in a game for the soul.

But there is a moral message that speaks today as loudly as it has ever done. In all these elements laid out before us the most important of all is the act of our own will.

The occultists tell us that the alchemical unions of which they speak are only empowered by the will of the adherent; the sexual serpent energy is nothing without the will-power of the one practising the rituals. God is nothing, we are told, without the will from the individual.

In the same way that Dracula cannot enter into our home unless we will it, Stoker tells us, quite plainly, that whatever we choose shall become our own reality.

The choice in *Dracula* is one of the dark Gothic old ways,

losing our sense of self, our life-blood and succumbing to its mystical charm or maintaining the traditional values of the Christian West and following the path of rationalism and science. The choice is as relevant today as it has always been.

As the man they called the anti-Christ, the occultist Aleister Crowley, was to say in the lifetime of Bram Stoker:

"Do what thou wilt shall be the whole of the Law."

Notes

[1] Ravenscroft, Trevor (1982). *The occult power behind the spear which pierced the side of Christ*. Red Wheel, p.165. ISBN 0877285470. These are rumours and the evidence is not forthcoming of membership. Regardless, it would not matter either way because Stoker was an excellent researcher and like Conan Doyle, an acquaintance, he utilised his research for fictional means.

Chapter 6

Bob Kane and the World of the Bats

In the world of Bram Stoker we found a battle of spirituality afoot in Victorian England. We discovered dark elements of psychology at play with archetypal images of serpents and bats. In the same way, the world of *Batman* conjures up concepts of the dark nature of man. It reveals a sense of foreboding found at the edges of our imagination. Yet it also tells a tale of hope and resurrection of the soul.

According to popular history the comic book stories of this dual natured individual were created by artist Bob Kane and writer Bill Finger, who in around 1939, grasped the rising current of collective hope on the brink of a world war and fostered a new Superman in the guise of Batman.

The story goes that the millionaire Bruce Wayne, so tormented by the violent death of his parents decides that he needs to take revenge upon the criminals of Gotham City and searches his mind for an answer. 'Suddenly, Wayne's thoughts were interrupted by a huge bat, which flickered through an open window near Wayne's armchair as if in response to some silent, unconscious summons. As it whirled and fluttered around his head – its silken wings etched sharply against the full moon which silently asserted its wan dominion over the murky night sky outside – Bruce Wayne realized that his grim musings had found their fulfilment. "A Bat" cried Wayne, "That's it! It's an omen. I shall become a Bat."' *Batman and Me,* Bob Kane and Tom Andrae, Eclipse Books, Forestville, Calif., p. 44

Wayne, following years of preparation, becoming a master scientist and training his mind and body, is now able to connect to his deeper, unconscious self and dark nature. He rises to the challenge from the depths of his unconscious cave and discovers a new creature of the night. In his conscious state, he struggles to deal with his own emotions and so takes on the mantle of his deeper state. He now feels that he must overcome his own fears and become the terror itself.

Held within the simple, comic book, tales created by two ordinary men before the Second World War, is a story with such depth that it has held the world spellbound ever since – for it talks to us all.

It is my opinion that the secret of the success of *Batman* is to be found within each and every one of us. It is archetypal – an inner representation of our own foreboding, not of the world outside ourselves, but the deeper, darker elements of our own mind.

Because this inner world is the same the world over, across cultures and across state boundaries, we shall discover that it is the element of the bat that shall be found to be one of the most powerful archetypal symbols of the dark nature of mankind. We shall also discover that this truth is not new, but instead something as ancient as man and his own consciousness.

The Tale of how Bob Kane originated *Batman*

Bob Kane was an ordinary guy who grew up in the Bronx in New York. He didn't have a privileged upbringing and certainly had to fight for everything that he could get. In many ways this explains the later, almost defensive stance he often took with regard to his creation of *Batman*, only later on in life mellowing slightly.

His own words reveal that he was well aware of his mortality. Revealing his own inner thoughts, as most writers do, he once said, "I believe that most people envy the immortality of a pop cult figure like Batman, who in his fictional world remains as young, handsome, and virile as he did when I created him. We all secretly fantasize that some of our superhero's fountain of youth will rub off on us." *Batman & Me*, Bob Kane and Tom Andrae, Eclipse Books, Forestville, Calif.

Kane was also aware of the subtle psychological world in which his consciousness would strive. He grew in a world that saw the rise and death of Sigmund Freud and Carl Jung – two of the founding fathers of modern psychology, who revealed the mystical elements of the deeper, unconscious self. These were concepts widely talked about as the young Kane absorbed the world around him. It was an age of discovery – not just of new science, but also of the mind of man. It was also an age of terror, as the occult Nazi party in Germany was set to terrorise the world.

Kane had an optimism grown out of his struggles as a youth and he even read Goethe, the German philosopher, explaining that Goethe's philosophy suited his own: "Whatever you can do or dream you can, begin it. Boldness has genius, power and magic in it. Begin it now." The truth is that Goethe never said these words or wrote them down and that the myth of these words has spread across the internet ever since. It seems they were mostly the words of a Scottish mountaineer called W. H. Murray.

These words attributed to Goethe, however, reveal one of the reasons that *Batman* has been so powerfully successful. It reveals that even in the dark side of the human mind, one can find optimism and strength. This is the defining moment in any human that he can find that *will* to go on and seek new heights, from the very depths of his own inner fear. *Batman* is the archetypal hero, because he is the physical manifestation of all our struggles and hopes, manifested against all our dark fears.

Luckily for Bob Kane, he intuitively knew what to do. He did not have to spend years of his life at the foot of the guru, or entrenched in the world of philosophy and religion, as many of us have to in order to discover our path. Very early on in life Kane set out his goals and with determined steely resolve he let nothing and no-one stand in his way.

A Dark crusader from within the dark nature of man himself.

By the time the Second World War had come around in Europe, and America was gearing itself up to join, Bob Kane had absorbed a number of important and influential elements that lead to the creation of Batman.

One of these was the dual nature and dual identity of the swashbuckling Zorro. During the daylight, Zorro was known as Don Diego Vega, a wealthy Mexican who at night turned into the masked crusader. The very term itself, Zorro, is Spanish for Fox, yet another nocturnal beast, like the bat.

Within the language of our fables, whether ancient or modern, there is often a clue to the almost subconscious mind of man manifesting within. Our words are created to have meaning and very often, later generations change and adapt these words, giving them new meanings. Yet, beneath the layers of these generations and additions we can still find the subtle truths, laid down as foundation stones for future times to discover. In this instance, it is pretty obvious that the man, Diego Vega, is the conscious self, fully aware of his surroundings and yet trapped, as we all are in the wheel of our own creating. We all have to work hard to survive and overcome the issues of the world we are trapped within.

However, Vega is one of the brightest stars in the sky – it is the awakened state, as opposed to the dreamy dark state of the night. It is the alter ego of the wily nocturnal fox or Zorro – the dual nature of man, revealed in the language of the past.

This, then, is a perfect starting point for the later pinnacle of dual-natured heroic characters – like Batman. Kane's mind was also racing with radio shows and stories such as *The Inner Sanctum, The Witch's Tale,* and of course, *The Shadow*. One phrase from *The Shadow* stayed with young Kane, so much so, that he had to include it within his own biography:

> "Who knows what evil lurks in the hearts of men… The Shadow knows…"

The Shadow is, of course, something that we cannot escape from.

In 1930 another influence played heavily upon Kane. A film by the name of *The Bat Whispers* was released; following an earlier attempt entitled just *The Bat*. It was based on a play also called *The Bat* by Avery Hopwood & Mary Hopkins Rinehart and has an unusual and deeply psychological story to tell.

A terror has fallen across the city, a masked criminal who goes by the name of The Bat. This criminal of the night raids the homes of millionaires and eludes the police. A rich socialite settles into a country mansion, where The Bat just happens to have stored his hoard and so our criminal goes on a killing spree to get at his loot from a secret room inside the house. However, the dark truth of this criminal's identity is revealed - to be one of the house guests. The dark nature it seems resides amongst us.

The Bat in his guise is remarkably like the Batman created by Kane. He wears a black bat mask, has bat wings and even reveals his symbol of the bat as a calling card as a silhouette in a glow of light upon the wall. The only difference is that Kane needed a hero and not a criminal.

However, this also reveals yet deeper and more thought provoking links for if Kane was influenced by *The Bat Whispers* then he must also have known of the influences upon that film. In 1915, Louis Feuillade released a silent film entitled *Les Vampires,* which was widely popular, eminently stylised and featured skulking masked villains. The depth of this influence, we shall soon see, reveals the ancient links to the unconscious torment within the dark mind of man.

Another interesting influence espoused by Kane himself and relevant today because of the infamous *Da Vinci Code* is the bird man drawn by the great artist, Leonardo da Vinci himself. In the words of Kane himself:

> *'The second influence was a Leonardo da Vinci book I had seen. The book had a lot of inventions, including a flying machine. It was a man on a sled like contraption with huge bat wings. Da Vinci had a quote that went something like, "Your bird will have no model but that of a bat." There it was – from a book 500 years old!' Batman and Me,* Bob Kane and Tom Andrae, Eclipse Books, Forestville, Calif.

This da Vinci flying machine is known as the ornithopter and does indeed look remarkably like a flying bat machine for man. There is even speculation that da Vinci actually got the thing to work.

However, it seems that the bat man concept, the dark nature and the bat wings had already previously been done in book, play and film, regardless of the images from a da Vinci drawing that Kane claims to have seen. The truth of the

The famous da Vinci flying machine which inspired Bob Kane.

matter is that this whole concept was not just inevitable; it had appeared for generations, taking twists and turns in the psyche of humanity.

As we will see below, one more influence, which opens up the world of the mind, played upon Kane's psyche – *Dracula*.

History

In 1938, the runaway success of Action Comics' *Superman* character prompted the National Publications, later DC Comics, to search for yet more superheroes. Together Bob Kane and Bill Finger created *Batman* and the ensuing arguments of who created exactly what have been ongoing ever since.

The very first Batman story finally arrived in May 1939 in *Detective Comics* (number 27) entitled *The Case of the Chemical Syndicate*. Many today would not recognise the more gritty element to *Batman*, who had no problem with killing or even maiming criminals and even had a gun. Nevertheless, *Batman* was an immediate success and by 1940 Batman had his own comic.

The huge success of *Superman* and *Batman* prompted a new genre and soon they were appearing together in the *World's*

Finest Comics by the 'fall' of 1940. At this time two additional writers were brought in, Jerry Robinson and Dick Sprang.

Over the coming months, and years, new elements were added into the tale of Batman, with stronger jaw lines and extended ears on the costume. The characteristic utility belt was added in July 1939 followed quickly by a batarang, a vehicle and the infamous origins of the Batmans dark natured past by September of the same year.

As early as November 1939 the rapidly softening edge of *Batman* resulted in the sidekick boy wonder, Robin, who also had a dual identity as Dick Grason. Robin was a warm hearted, but tough, teenager and ward of Bruce Wayne. He is described as the daredevil young aide and young laughing Robin Hood of the day. He is also impatient, foolhardy, reckless and the living hurricane. All of this in stark contrast to the controlled and logical mind of Batman made for a perfect union and interesting tale. Sales of the comics nearly doubled overnight and other newly created superheroes quickly followed suit.

From the very start two of the most infamous adversaries to the dynamic duo were introduced - the Joker and Catwoman - and by 1942 almost all of the now easily recognisable elements of *Batman* had been formed. By the end of the Second World War however, the darker side of Batman in his bleak and menacing world were being stripped out in favour of a more optimistic approach - reflecting the cultural movements and feelings in the world at large.

By the 1950's interest in superheroes was waning, but *Batman* remained and in 1952 he joins forces with *Superman* in the tale *The Mightiest Team in the World*, where these dual personalities discover each others true identities. This sparked a renewed interest and pretty soon Batman and Superman were regularly featured together - right up until 1986.

In this new post-war world of innovation there was a distinct excitement among the general Western population for all things modern and specifically scientific. This created a desire to imagine a better future and so *Batman* tales became positively more science fiction based. Space aliens and bizarre scientific creations are set against the superheroes. However, by 1964 *Batman* sales were plummeting and DC Comics, according to Bob Kane, were set to kill him off altogether.

But then a new editor was brought in, Julius Schwartz and

radically changed Batman. In May 1964, the 'New Look' Batman was revealed with a return to detective style tales and the introduction of the famous Batmobile, not to mention the new design costume with the introduction of the yellow ellipse behind the Bat insignia. Almost all the 1950's science fiction based characters were sent into oblivion and even the much loved butler, Alfred, was killed off and replaced with Aunt Harriet.

In 1966 Adam West debuted as Batman in the hit TV series which also saw Alfred back from the dead and introduced the feminine principle of Batgirl into a world ever more conscious of the general sexual inequalities. The TV show inevitably influenced the comics themselves, but by as early as 1968, after only two years the show was cancelled and the comics once again began to decline.

It was decided in 1969, mainly by writers Dennis O'Neill and Neal Adams that the camp nature of the TV show and the copycat comic editions had caused the downslide and so they returned Batman back to his original state as the grim avenger of the night.

By 1970 a stream of writers collaborated on recreating Bob Kane's and Bill Finger's original ideas and the result was a return to the more darker elements of the Batman theme, so loved by fans across the world. However popularity still decreased regardless, hitting an all-time low by 1985.

Then in 1986 Frank Miller introduced a limited edition series entitled *Batman – the Dark Knight Returns*. This is the story of, the now 50-year old, Bruce Wayne coming out of retirement to fight the modern day criminals. It was a huge success and led to Dennis O'Neil and others recreating the younger Batman in a similar dark vein, even retelling his origins and the death of his parents. Because of the darker edge now introduced into the Batman tales a new older generation became interested and with the addition of movies a whole new reviatlised cult following emerged.

Today *Batman* has yet again been recreated with even grittier, more realistic and psychologically-dark, tales and a new success story is unravelling. What tomorrow may bring for our Dark Knight we cannot say, but judging from history it will certainly follow the underlying psychology of the general population at large. And this has been true of not just *Batman*, but also the precursors of Batman – the Vampire.

The Vampire

As we have already discovered in *Dracula*, the vampire has been part of the human subconscious for a very long time. In modern popular folklore the vampire is evil, with intent upon taking our very soul and sapping our life-blood in order to survive. These concepts are deeply rooted in the fear of the unconscious mind - the dark recesses of our very selves.

The vampire is clearly related to the bat and so we ought to begin our dig with this little creature.

Looking at the language, as we did with the vampire (fire before) we discover that bat derives from the word bakka, as in the Swedish nattbakke or night bat. Bakka is related to much more ancient concepts and means the land of light or fire. As we found in the previous chapter the sacred heart of Islam, Mecca, was once known as Bakka, because it holds the starry stones that fell from heaven - the light of the night sky falling to the ground and which are now kept in a perfectly black state like the night itself. Here we are finding that the bat was not something of evil, but a carrier or transition device between the world of man and the world of the deities. It traversed the twilight, it overcame the fear we humans had of the night and therefore had preference to the light or fire.

This fire spoken of by our ancestors was a unique experience, enabled from within the dark recesses of the mind known as the illumination, the fire within. Man would struggle with his fear, overcome it and delve within the unconscious self to access the divine. In fact this is the very same serpentine energy system spoken of by Paracelsus, the alchemists and fought against in *Dracula* by Bram Stoker.

The power of utilising this "magical" energy was given to shaman, who were said to take flight and gave rise to the Greek ferryman of the river Styx known as the Charon - meaning to fly. Later this Charon became a coin, used to pay for the dead to access the otherworld or Hades. We have a whole new meaning now to the phrase "like a bat out of hell."

In fact, these were remnants of a pre-Christian era that worshipped the serpent and utilized various methods of finding the fire within, including blood rituals and ecstatic states. This place of peace within ones own mind was known to the Hindu's as the void - a metaphysical concept not easily understood in the classical Christian sense.

The winged serpent or dragon is a universally accepted archetype, as is the bat. There are physical reasons and internal psychological reasons, but important to our research here is the fact that they were creatures of both the physical night and the mental night. As the Dark Knight, Batman was the ultimate union between the dragon-bat and man himself. He battles for the light, whilst sinking into the deep dark night.

Bob Kane may very well have been subconsciously fulfilling his own inner wishes and desires on paper when he created Batman. He may have been placing his alter ego within the folds of the caped crusader. As he himself said:

> *"I surmise that my fantasies are shared by most people – and therein lies the key to* Batman's *longevity and success." Batman and Me,* Bob Kane and Tom Andrae, Eclipse Books, Forestville, Calif.

This is the very essence of the process – a work on the self, a wish to be a better person and to overcome ones own fears. Kane's troubled boyhood fights and losses emerged as the victorious super hero, but this only turned the tables of a negative image for the bat into something much more profound. The deeper insight comes when we understand that the dark knight emerged from a universal and archetypal link within ourselves.

Bob Kane and Bill Finger, whilst absorbing the cultural influences surrounding them in the early twentieth century, revised and re-created the shaman who does battle for humanity. They admitted that they intuitively pulled archetypes from within their own minds and merged them into the greatest of super heroes. They turned the world of propaganda on its head and gave back to the bat its special place in our hearts and minds. What we shall never now know is whether Kane and Finger were truly conscious of what they had really done.

Batman, in one form or another, shall go on as long as man exists, because he is the drive, the fear, the tormentor, pressing us forward and goading us towards the light of a new dawn.

> *'Wayne's thoughts were interrupted by a huge bat, which flickered through an open window near Wayne's armchair as if in response to some silent, unconscious summons.' Batman and Me,* Bob Kane and Tom Andrae, Eclipse Books, Forestville, Calif.

Chapter 7

Sir Arthur Conan Doyle - Even the Wise Get Confused

Fantastic worlds of science fiction, mysterious ancient arts of alchemy and modern super heroes all emerging from the mind of man. All these men providing us with entertainment, enlightenment and stark warnings of what lies within ourselves. For me however, the ultimate symbol of the battle between our own desires, fears and needs is to be found in the author of the popular Sherlock Holmes novels - Sir Arthur Conan Doyle.

There is a concept of the ultimate logical human being, copied by generations of writers for decades. The famous Spock of *Star Trek* is but one example of man overcoming his emotional frailties to emerge into the cold world of logic. However we must remember that the most popular of these cold-blooded characters is but one element from within the mind of a man who had a fascinating background, committed much of his life in search of the occult and ended his days mocked by society.

Many authors throughout time have stumbled upon the world of the occult and included it within their work as we have discovered. One of these is the author who created the ultimate logical detective, Sherlock Holmes.

Born Arthur Ignatius Conan Doyle on 22nd May 1859 he was a prolific Scottish author and medical practitioner. He was sent to a Roman Catholic Jesuit preparatory school where he was indoctrinated into the mystical world of the Catholic religion.

Following this, he went to Stonyhurst Jesuit College and by leaving school in 1875 he was a declared agnostic, rejecting Christianity outright. Before moving on to University he was sent to yet another Jesuit school in Austria known as the Stella Matutina - a name meaning morning star and also used for the Temple of the Golden Dawn secret occult society frequented by many of the great and good. This appears to have been a somewhat happier experience and he particularly enjoyed reading, stating that Edgar Allan Poe's *Tales of Mystery and Imagination* was a profound influence upon him just as Poe had been to Verne. Poe was also a great influence on the James

Arthur Conan Doyle.

Bond author, Ian Fleming, who was also schooled in Austria (see *The Bond Code*, Philip Gardiner, New Page Books, 2008). Importantly author Harold Bloom described Poe once as 'the American Gnostic' due to his mystical and metaphysical leanings.

The Jesuit connections with Doyle would later in life lose him parliamentary elections for being a *"Papist conspirator, a Jesuit emissary, and a Subverter of the Protestant Faith." (The Hound of the Baskervilles : another adventure of Sherlock Holmes,* by Arthur Conan Doyle, Sir Christopher Frayling, Penguin, 2002) Somebody, it seems, suspected that there was more to Conan Doyle than met the eye.

Interestingly, the Jesuit order gave rise to the infamous secret society, called the Illuminati, which was also founded in Austria, under Adam Weishaupt, less than a hundred years before Doyle's time there. The Jesuits themselves have been called the Gestapo of the Catholic Church. With their spidery web across the world, infiltrating all-manner of religious, commercial, political and charitable institutions they would often take on a guise that would make them unrecognisable. There is little wonder that Doyle would later predict that 'the forms of religion will be abandoned, but the essence will be maintained; so that one universal creed will embrace the whole civilized earth'. http://www.spiritwritings.com/arthurconandoyle.html

However, from 1876 until 1881 Doyle studied medicine at Edinburgh and upon achieving his goal he celebrated by drawing a sketch of himself waving his diploma with the caption:

'Licensed to Kill'.

It is thought that this was indeed where Ian Fleming got the title for his later Bond book.

Doyle moved on and set up a medical practice in Portsmouth, which gave him a comfortable income after the first few years. During this period he continued writing stories in his spare time. The most famous of these are of course the tales of the detective Sherlock Holmes and within the folds of these and other complex narratives we find elements of the occult that so fascinated Doyle. In fact, the occult references are so strong that his short story collection *The Adventures of Sherlock Holmes*, was actually banned from the Soviet Union in 1929 for their supposed occultism. The ban was eventually lifted.

The forms of the occult influence that seeped into the Doyle novels took a great many shapes. In an early work entitled *The Mystery of Cloomber* we find a trio of Buddhist monks having returned from the dead seeking revenge upon an army officer. Every chapter is filled to the brim with manifestations of the paranormal for example:

> *"...astral projection, precognition, extrasensory perception and even matter transmission." The Mystery of Cloomber*, Sir Arthur Conan Doyle, http://www.gutenberg.org/etext/7964

This matter transmission was the concept of resolving objects into their base chemical atoms and then compelling them to take their original form. It was, in essence a scientific language for the metaphor of alchemy – Doyle's mind making the spiritual seem logical. Sometime later Doyle wrote *The Doings of Raffles Haw,* which centred around the secret of alchemy itself and indeed mirrors the words of occultist Eliphas Levi in his book *The Great Secret*.

> *"This is the great secret. It is the secret, which endows man who knows it with such a universal power as no man has ever enjoyed since the world was made. This secret it is the dearest wish of my heart to use for good, and I swear to you, Robert McIntyre, that if I thought it would tend to anything but good I would have done with it forever." The Doings of Raffles Haw,* Sir Arthur Conan Doyle.

Unfortunately, along with *The Mystery of Cloomber*, this book has been placed amongst what are termed Doyle's most obscure works. And next to nothing remains of the details of his lonely visit to the Coptic Monastery at the Natron Lakes in Egypt - a Christian sect with distinctly Gnostic leanings. He rode fifty miles into the desert in searing heat, spending several days away from his ailing wife in Cairo. This kind of effort is not taken lightly, I know.

In essence, Doyle was playing out his own thoughts and beliefs on the pages of the novels. He was deeply interested in the occult world, in the paranormal and myths. In 1898 he went along to the Temple of the Hermetic Order of the Golden Dawn, a group closely linked with the Theosophical Society and the Rosicrucian's, who themselves were linked to the Illuminati of Austria and groups that also heavily influenced Ian Fleming.

However it is claimed that Conan Doyle found the goings on to be "queer and disagreeable" and so never went again. Strange then, that Doyle later made his home at Crowborough, the very home of the Grand Lodge of Rosicrucianism, and that members I have spoken to claim that he was, in fact, an initiate of the same degree as Madame Blavatsky, Eliphas Levi and the beast himself Aleister Crowley. It seems, he was attracted to these societies for his very real interest in the paranormal, and not the bizarre rituals and petty politics that often came with them. That said, at his home in the New Forest known as Bignell House, the postman declined to visit because of the strange goings on and the local villagers avoided it because of the spiritualist activities.

He did however join the Society for Psychical Research and lectured extensively on the subjects of the paranormal and occult. The world of the hidden was to be in more than just the realm of fiction for Doyle. He is noted for his acceptance of the Cottingley Fairies, which later proved to be pure fiction themselves.

Conan Doyle died in 1930 and was highly influential upon the minds of a great many including Bob Kane, H. G. Wells and Ian Fleming, as we have seen. They had similar circles of friends, which included Winston Churchill, and they all wrote upon the world of the occult.

Like Bond, Sherlock Holmes would have his own nemesis in Professor Moriarty and his "happy helper" in Dr Watson.

And yet he would also suffer from the depressions of loneliness, smoke too much and dabble in his cocaine habit. Once he even met his perfect feminine principle or Gnostic Sophia who was a match for him. Doyle opened himself up to what he saw as the real world with his beliefs in the paranormal, fairies and psychics and paid the price of humiliation.

The Esoteric World of Conan Doyle

Arthur Conan Doyle was born into an Irish Catholic family at Picardy Place, Edinburgh, on 22nd. May 1859. His father, Charles Altamont Doyle, a civil servant in the Edinburgh Office of Works, suffered from epilepsy, was an alcoholic, and died in an asylum in 1893. There is evidence to suggest that his mother, Mary Foley, had openly taken a lover, Dr. Bryan Charles Waller, as a lodger. Doyle would play down this element of his mother's life, and yet Mary continued to live with Waller for the remainder of her days.

Arthur Conan Doyle.

It was the same Dr. Waller who influenced Doyle to pursue a medical career, rather than follow in the family tradition of artists and painters, qualifying from Edinburgh University in 1885. He first set up a practice with a fellow student, Dr Budd, in Plymouth but later moved to Southsea with his new wife Louisa, following some moralistic disagreements. Here he established himself as an eye specialist. It was also here that between 1885 and 1888 he attended a number of spiritual 'table turning' sittings at the home of General Drayson.

In 1887 he joined the Society for Psychical Research and the Freemasons at the age of 27. Among those present was Dr James Watson, with whom Doyle became very friendly, and whose name has been immortalised in the Holmes stories.

Doyle rose rapidly through the degrees and was passed to the second degree on 23rd. February 1887 and a month later he became a Master Mason. It seems however that his swift rise to Master Mason left him feeling empty – as if the Masons had little more to give this man on a quest, and so he resigned in 1889. There is evidence to suggest that Doyle was a little perturbed with some of the false claims of Freemasonry.

However the journey to find his own truth was not over and so he continued to attend Lodge meetings as an unattached Mason and even rejoined, finally leaving in 1911 after receiving several Masonic honors. In 1900 he was even made an honorary member of the Lodge at Edinburgh.

The year of his joining the Freemasons, 1887, strangely coincided with his introduction of Sherlock Holmes. *A Study in Scarlet* was released in the Beeton's Christmas Annual and in reading the many tales of Sherlock Holmes, and indeed other tales, we find that there are several references to Freemasonry:

In *The Adventure of the Norwood Builder* from 1903 we have:

> 'You mentioned your name as if I should recognize it, but beyond the obvious facts that you are a bachelor, a solicitor, a Freemason, and an asthmatic, I know nothing whatever about you.'

In *The Adventure of the Red-Headed League* from 1891 we have:

> 'Beyond the obvious facts that he has at some time done manual labour, that he takes snuff, that he is a Freemason.

That he has been in China, and that he has done a considerable amount of writing lately, I can deduce nothing else.'

'Well, the snuff, then, and the Freemasonry?'

'I won't insult your intelligence by telling you how I read that, especially as, rather against the strict rules of your order, you use an arc-and-compass breastpin.'

In *The Land of Mist*, Doyle expresses what may have been his own thoughts – that Freemasonry no longer held any great mystery for him:

"He is one of those who wander about on the obscure edges of Masonry, talking with whispers and reverence of mysteries where no mystery is. Spiritualism, with its very real and awful mysteries, is, to him, a vulgar thing because it brought consolation to common folk, but he loves to read papers on the Palladian Callus, ancient and accepted Scottish rites and baphometic figures. Eliphas Levi is his prophet. "

The truth is, that Conan Doyle was searching for answers to his own inner questions and the seemingly mystical and mythological world of the Freemasons was just one place he searched. Throughout his life, Doyle spread his wings and questioned the weird and wonderful, unafraid to openly express his own desire to know and his own beliefs. The *Land of Mist* is a book sacred to the Theosophists that I have spoken to because it reveals cleverly the concepts of other planes of existence and our own true path within the realm we inhabit. One quotation alone demonstrates this:

'Children are not born here. That is only on the earth plane. It was this aspect of marriage to which the great Teacher referred when he said: "There will be neither marriage nor giving in marriage". No! It is purer, deeper, more wonderful, a unity of souls, a complete merging of interests and knowledge without a loss of individuality. The nearest you ever get to it is the first high passion, too beautiful for physical expression when two high-souled lovers meet upon your plane. They find lower expression afterwards, but they will always in their hearts know that the first delicate, exquisite soul-union was the more lovely. So it is with us.' *The Land of Mist,* Sir Arthur Conan Doyle.

This is an expression, beautifully put, of the uniting of the Gnostic truths. Of the male and female counterparts, strength and wisdom, forming a perfect union in a higher realm. Doyle goes on to express that those who have formed balance or union of these twin principles must not remain in the higher plane, but must help those who are still in the lower realms. This is the avatar, the angel, the wise ones of ancient times, taught in the mystery schools and within the Freemasonic brotherhoods. It is in fact the root principle of the Masonic world – the fraternity, the helping one another and this is why Doyle sped up the ranks so swiftly.

The reason that he was so inspired by the American Gnostic, Edgar Allen Poe, and why he visited the Gnostic Copts in Egypt is simple, because Conan Doyle included this ancient wisdom within his own tales. A Gnostic is one who by mystical knowledge has a sense of the Divine within the self and this, from the first century onwards set them against the ruling Christian order. Conan Doyle, from early on, had rejected Catholicism and even went against his own family by openly stating his agnosticism. He did however have an inner sense of spirituality that he struggled with for many years, finally coming to the conclusion that there was life after death, that the rule of any politically oriented religious organization was not right and that there was more to the mystical experience than he had previously thought. The logic of Sherlock Holmes was therefore in stark contrast to the creator and yet also part of himself.

The knowledge of Conan Doyle, revealed in the expanse of his works, shows that he had read widely on the subject of the occult in order to come to terms with his inner turmoil between logic and spirit. His reference to Eliphas Levi in *The Land of Mist*, shows quite clearly that he knew of the current surge in the world of the occult and he even revealed this in other works.

There is also a little-known translation by Conan Doyle of a sacred alchemical text called the *Nuctemeron*, the origin of which is very unclear. Apollonius of Tyre, a teacher from the school of Pythagoras, is often mentioned as the author. The earliest publication in Greek is by Lorenzo de Mosheim in Amsterdam in 1721. It became better known through the translation by none other than Eliphas Levi in his *Dogma and Ritual of Magic*. The English translation however was by Sir

Arthur Conan Doyle and is based on Levi's version, revealing that Doyle read Levi's work. The *Nuctemeron* describes in a powerful and ornate style, the transfiguration of the human soul. It was intended that it penetrate deeply into the essence of the soul with every step taken, ending in the twelfth hour when the deeds of light are done.

We have to remember, that this was a time when many mystery movements were stirring in the world, trying to find answers to the age-old questions without having to turn to the priest. One of these was Theosophy and Doyle was very closely associated with them, as was Eliphas Levi and as suggested above in fact *The Land of Mist* is a Theosophical work of great repute. Just like Stoker, Doyle walked in the realms of mystery societies and produced works of fiction from their influence. Both writers understood the darker elements of these peculiar anti-Christian worlds and both writers knew also that there was some truth held within. And yet Stoker and Doyle part company when we arrive at the world of the spirits.

Arthur Conan Doyle with Harry Houdini.

Almost all these societies were interested in spiritualism – contacting the dead. In fact at this period it was not something overly mocked, with many of the great and good sharing in the supposedly new concepts. One of Doyle's own friends in the Psychical Research Society was Arthur Balfour, a future Prime Minister of England. It was, in effect, a search for truth – something Doyle said to be of the greatest importance. It was the search in a non-religious way for a meaning to life itself.

In his very public searching, Doyle famously made friends with the American illusionist, Harry Houdini, and they remained friends for many years. Houdini was himself fascinated with the world of spiritualism and the occult, collecting huge amounts of literature from Levi to the infamous occultist, alchemist, Freemason and to some, impostor, Cagliostro. Eventually the clash of Doyle's belief and Houdini's logical impulse distanced them somewhat. However, on Houdini's death, Conan Doyle spoke of the sad loss of this great magician:

> 'Be his mystery what it may, Houdini was one of the most remarkable men of whom we have any record, and he will live in history with such personalities as Cagliostro, the Chevalier D'Eon, and other strange characters.' *The Edge of the Unknown*, Sir Arthur Conan Doyle, 1930.

It is strange enough that Houdini be compared with Cagliostro, but stranger still that he be compared to Chevalier D'Eon, who was a spy, a Freemason and was even suspected of being female. What Doyle saw in his Freemasonic brother, Houdini, was a depth of knowledge and a will to find the truth – a modern alchemist. However with ideas that Houdini may have spied for the US government and his lack of sex drive towards females, we may have a little more of the truth stated here by Doyle than Houdini would have liked.

However, these great ideals and intentions can and have often, lead well-meaning people up the garden path, to where the fairies reside.

Fairies

Anybody who knows about Sir Arthur Conan Doyle will be aware of the period in his life that seems most at odds with Sherlock Holmes – the Cottingley Fairies.

The Cottingley Fairies were named after the small town in England where two young girls claimed to have seen and to even play with fairies. Nobody believed them and so they borrowed a camera and took several pictures. Still nobody believed them, until a photography expert was asked to take a look by a leading Theosophist, Edward Gardner. The expert, Fred Barlow, actually confirmed that the photographs were very real and, as luck would have it, Conan Doyle had been commissioned by *The Strand* magazine to write an article on fairies and so became heavily involved through his Theosophical links.

How can it be that the creator of Sherlock Holmes - a detective who dealt in facts, not theories, and who refused to acknowledge that the supernatural could exist - could himself have believed in fairies, and could have been duped by two young girls into publicly declaring that their photographs of fairies were real?

The most often used excuse for this is Doyle's relationship with Spiritualism and the Theosophists, which, it is claimed derived from the death of his son, Kingsley in 1918. However Conan Doyle had expressed his beliefs in Spiritualism well before his son's death and had experimented with table turning in 1885. The truth is that Fairies were part of Doyle's make-up, internally from his youth, and his desire to find evidence for their existence due to his logical / medical mind lead him into error.

As he later wrote:

> *"My heart was gladdened when out here in far Australia I had your note and the three wonderful pictures which are confirmatory of our published results. When our fairies are admitted other psychic phenomena will find a more ready acceptance ... we have had continued messages at seances for some time that a visible sign was coming through..."* http://en.wikipedia.org/wiki/Cottingley_Fairies

Conan Doyle was born into a family that was well-known for its artistic abilities and yet he turned the tables and opted for medicine. Richard Doyle, his uncle, was the designer of the infamous *Punch* magazine cover and a notable artist of the weird and wonderful. The *Punch* cover was festooned with fairy-folk.

Richard Doyle from the very start had loved the world of

folklore. He spent his time in the world of the imagination with elves, goblins, fairies, and sprites. One particular journal entry explains to our modern, psychologically inclined minds exactly what was occurring. He claimed openly that, when he was young, he was kept awake by strange visions as he lay in bed. He was visited by gnomes and fairies and try as he might, he could not stay awake long enough to draw them.

This world that Doyle's uncle speaks of is the world of the mystic. It is the world that lies at the point between awake and asleep (hypnagogic/hypapompic). It is the dark world of the mind, bringing forth images from the unconscious world into our very consciousness. Whatever is placed within the folds of the dark fabric of the unconscious world is from everyday experience and indeed from possible quantum connection to the universe itself. These images and thoughts, sights and sounds, often find a way of expressing themselves to our conscious mind. These gateways into our world are dreams or lucid dreaming, where we are neither awake, nor asleep.

We need not imagine that Conan Doyle was toying with these concepts, because he wrote about them, specifically in *The Leather Funnel*. In this interesting esoteric tale, Doyle has his character sleep with a peculiar leather funnel artifact, so that he may understand its true origin from within his sleeping state. The hero does indeed enter a world of darkness, which he describes as hell, but nevertheless retrieves the information desired. It is the journey of the shaman spoken of thousands of times. It is the journey into another world.

This world, is the one that mystics have utilized for thousands of years to supposedly connect with the Divine. It is in the sleepless state that angels, demons, aliens and ghosts are seen. The world of the mystic is beautiful and yet hellish, for what we find is what we are and what we take with us. Indeed, it is the same world of the serpent energy to which we have constantly been returning.

Often, these experiences are extreme and can cause mental disturbances. Sometimes these mental disturbances were brought on purposefully, such as in the case of Sherlock Holmes who abuses cocaine and some biographers assert that Doyle himself may have taken the drug to see better into the otherworld. In Doyle's day, although taking cocaine was legal and widespread, the effects often caused severe mental breakdown that was classed as madness and lunacy and unless you overcame the problem, then you would find yourself in an insane asylum.

This is precisely what happened to that other great artist, Charles Doyle, Conan Doyle's father. In one of his sketchbooks, he wrote:

> 'Keep steadily in view that this book is ascribed wholly to the produce of a madman.' http://bjp.rcpsych.org/cgi/content/full/191/6/A22

It was both Charles Doyle's artistic influence and Uncle Richard's that would play upon the mind of young Arthur.

The very speed with which Arthur Conan Doyle could write stories and the creativity and fluidity of his work, could now easily be put down to his inner connection to his own unconscious self. He was an open gateway, just like his father and uncle and experienced mystical, occult impulses that are evidenced by his life-long search for the truth.

Arthur Conan Doyle was drawn to the world of the esoteric and Gnostic thought, because he experienced thoughts and visions just like the members of his own family. This, in turn leads one to wonder on the genetic link, which has been proven by modern science to be real, that Conan Doyle was mystically inclined due to his own heritage.

The Theosophical Society, founded by such mystics, and some would say fraudsters, as Madam Blavatsky, was deeply interested in the esoteric and Gnostic world. It is even claimed that Blavatsky herself aided Conan Doyle and that he sought her mediumship skills. There is little wonder that, later on in his life, he was drawn by his friends in the Theosophy Society to the infamous Cottingley Fairies and the tale of how two little girls took a few photographs and fooled the genius creator of Sherlock Holmes. Had Bram Stoker seen this element of the Eastern cults taking over his peer? It most certainly was no secret.

So Who Was Sherlock Holmes and Why?

Can we uncover more of the mind of Conan Doyle by deciphering the fictional man he created? Just who did Conan Doyle base his most infamous of characters upon? Was there a detective sleuth at large that formed the basis of this most famous of fictional characters? Or did he simply spring from the mind of the creator?

The truth is to be found on many levels. Most people who know anything about Conan Doyle will know that his teacher at Edinburgh University, Joseph Bell, bore a striking physical resemblance to the later creation, quite apart from the fact that he taught the art of deduction. Even Sir Arthur himself made this assertion. And so we have one side of Sherlock in this university lecturer, but what about the solid anti-spiritualist aspect revealed by Doyle?

Well, there was a man, whom Conan Doyle would meet later in life and whom he had admired for many years. He had spoken out against spiritualism, calling it a plague and saying that 'spiritualism is quietly undermining the traditional ideas of the future state.'[1] His name was Oliver Wendell Holmes.

Like Conan Doyle, Wendell Holmes was a physician and he was the pinnacle of the logical element that Doyle admired, stating 'I saw, as a medical man, how a spicule of bone or a tumor pressing on the brain, would cause what seemed an alteration of the soul.' This revealed his own inner sense of conflict. On the one hand he had been brought up in a family that sensed more, with a mother who read him tales of legend and myth, an uncle who saw fairies and painted them and a father who resided in an insane asylum until the end of his days because of his inability to deal with his own visions. And yet, his medical training and the influence of Joseph Bell and Wendell Holmes forced home the facts and figures, the science and scrutiny.

This turmoil had to be worked out and, like most writers, Conan Doyle did so on paper. Sherlock Holmes became a mixture of the mind of Doyle himself with all his life's influences. He struggled with his own inner feelings and almost mystical experiences and yet balanced them sufficiently to create fictional works of pure genius. Sherlock fought the foolish notions of spiritualism and yet Dr Watson questioned, …'was God fearing and open?.' Their constant dialogue reveals the inner voice of Conan Doyle himself, the dark and the light at war, whereby one side shall win, or an equilibrium be found. In Doyle's case he fought the battle for many years and finally succumbed in the end to a little of both.

However there was another character introduced by Doyle, which revealed his own darker emotions – Professor Moriarty.

Anybody who knows of this infamous character will know

that he is an evil genius, with almost the exact opposite mind and role as Sherlock Holmes. He is the Gnostic darkness, sent to test the light, to re-unite. In fact, Moriarty's Christian name is James, and the Gnostic belief was that James was not just the brother of Jesus the light, but also the twin. Fair hair or golden locks were a physical symbol of the one who was the light, and of course, Sherlock simply means bright haired.

It is fitting in this respect, that Sherlock himself should die, supposedly entwined with Moriarty, at the Reichenbach falls, only to be resurrected alchemically like the phoenix of legend.

Moriarty bears too many close resemblances to Conan Doyle, being in a sense a wraith-like spectre of himself. He is born in Ireland, from where the Doyle family originated, and has many of Doyle's self-beliefs. In the words of Doyle himself:

> 'He is a genius, a philosopher, an abstract thinker.'

According to Inspector MacDonald of Scotland Yard in *The Valley of Fear*, Moriarty was like a father figure, very talented and they spoke about eclipses. This was a subtle clue laid down by Doyle – as the eclipse is when the light and dark come together.

And yet, said Doyle, Moriarty had dark tendencies, hereditary and diabolical tendencies. A criminal strain ran in his blood. The madness in the Doyle family found literary life.

This darkness within Conan Doyle is the turmoil, the chaos of the conflict between logic and spirit, conscious and unconscious, and is revealed in his own words:

> 'I had everything in those few years to make a man contented. And yet my soul was often troubled within me. I felt that I was born for something else, and yet I was not clear what that something might be. My mind felt out continually into the various religions of the world. I could no more get into the old ones, as commonly received, than a man could get into a boy's suit.' *Teller of Tales: The Life of Sir Arthur Conan Doyle*, Daniel Stashower, Owl Books, New York, 1999.

This statement speaks of a turning point in Doyle's life, a time when he resurrects Holmes and a time when he steps more boldly into the world of the spirit. He begins to agree more wholeheartedly with the future Prime Minister, Arthur Balfour, when he said in paraphrasing Shakespeare:

'...there are things in heaven and earth not hitherto dreamed of in our scientific philosophy.' *The Journal of Philosophy, Psychology and Scientific Methods*, Vol. 7, No. 22 (Oct. 27, 1910), pp. 589 -594.

It seems also in the words placed into the mouth of Sherlock Holmes that Doyle was revealing a little of himself:

'My mind rebels at stagnation. Give me problems, give me work, give me the most abstruse cryptogram, or the most intricate analysis, and I am in my own proper atmosphere. But I abhor the dull routine of existence. I crave for mental exaltation.' *Teller of Tales: The Life of Sir Arthur Conan Doyle*, Daniel Stashower, Owl Books, New York, 1999.

Conan Doyle worked out the Gnostic and even Jesuit influences that he had been party to on the pages of his novels. In *The Hound of the Baskervilles* there is a satanic force and Grimpen Mire, where the tale is set, is in fact derived from Anglo-Saxon for the Devil. This is the return of Sherlock, written years after Doyle had killed him off. Here he enters the dark hellish world and struggles against the dark nature.

Doyle would in the end find his mental exaltation in the realm of the spirits and the unknown.

Ancient Wisdom

What Doyle was searching for, found and relayed to us in the many tales he told is ancient wisdom. It is knowledge of the mind of man from within the mind of man, worked out for generations and placed in the sacred texts and symbols of the world by all-manner of cultures. Doyle believed he was guided by one of the ancients by the name of Pheneas, whom his second wife communicated with. Pheneas was an Arab scribe from Ur in ancient Sumeria – a concept much alive within the Theosophical movement at the time and still very much to this day.

However, all these cultures have come to the same conclusions about ourselves, not because they all emerged from some sunken Atlantis or ancient astronaut, but because all our minds work on the same principles.

Doyle, as a member of the Freemasons, Psychical Research Society and in all likelihood a regular visitor to the

Theosophical Society, would have gathered these facts, for they are taught within most mystery schools.

The truths lead us not into science, nor spirit, but to nature and intuition. To a place within the self that is open and free to allow our natural self to speak out. By working through these ancient processes, Doyle was attempting to overcome what he himself had become - confused. The process clears confusion, balances out the fire and water of our natures and allows the creative spark to ignite a pure flame.

Often those who have experienced the very real and human mystical moment of lucid dreaming are left with a sense of needing to know more. Add to this a family of creative people, the myth and fantasy stories of the mother, the mysticism of the Catholic and Jesuit world, and we are left with deep desires. Desires to find answers to the many conflicts that arise in the mind of a man who is being taught science and the art of deduction, whilst all the time experiencing what were to him, very real events.

Logical deduction, scientific analysis and detective genius ran alongside myth, mystery and mysticism for Conan Doyle and he needed to square this circle. He did so in the end by becoming a religious fanatic for spiritualism and lost many friends in so doing - but he was at least settled in his new belief.

The end result was a lifetime of literary works, some bizarre and some beautiful, some crazy and some creative, but always signposts along the way for a man who was walking a path to discovery.

Today we can look back at these signs and see moments from the mind of Doyle and how he struggled with his own emotions and thoughts. We can see how he merged the mythological world with the cold world of reality and in that fusion he created an eternal story that speaks to us all, because it is a caricature of our lives, regardless of the period in which we live.

The subtle and friendly battles between Holmes and Watson are but the balance of perfection within our minds that must be found if we are to solve the riddles of existence.

Notes

1 http://www.todancewithangels.com/meeting_of_the_minds.htm

Chapter 8

Magic, Mind, God

There are many things we can learn from our foray into the world of these diverse men. Of these many things, I wish to focus in on the mystical world, the magical world, the strange and wonderful, that each of them has somehow managed to find contact.

Magic is the belief that the material universe is only a very minor part of all reality and that it includes many other planes of existence and even consciousness. In the same way we possess consciousness and unconsciousness – both of which have their own concepts of reality – so too the Universe mirrors this and more. In the same way we cannot access the unconscious realm of our own mind, we simply cannot access the other realities of the Universe – unless of course there is a way? And that is the realm of magic – being able to find ways of accessing other realities and affect our own. One of the other "realms" or "realities" of magic is known as the astral light and believers of this reality say that the cosmic fluid of the astral light can form or mold physical forms. The force that can do this is said to be human thought, human will-power. The human being, existing in the microcosm can, once it understands, affect the macrocosm – the small can affect the large. We can set in motion an action in our level of reality and cause an affect in the greater reality.

All of this can sound quite potty to the mind that is not used to such concepts and like the hand of a clock we need to adjust our position a moment at a time in order to understand that time and things change. Understanding this magical ability of the human being takes some effort and, indeed, it has taken men lifetimes either to come to terms with it, or blow it away altogether. In essence, man discovers that he is in fact God in almost every sense of the word.

To the growing elite and occult brotherhoods magic was truly powerful. One famous 19th and early 20th century occultist was Dr Gerard Encausse otherwise known as Papus. He founded the modern group known as the Martinists, based upon an 18th century Martinist Order, a kind of New Age Christian sect. He claimed that magic was really scientific, carrying out experiments on powers and energies that were little understood at the time. He stated that magic was dangerous, and that three main principles were required in its operation, namely the will-power of the individual, the actual material basis (the tool) and the actual force upon which the mind or will operates and affects a change in the material. This was a period seeing the rise in scientific thought overpowering the religious or the spiritual but Martinists and others, (such as the Rosicrucians) saw a middle ground. This force, which science would discover, was known to the Jews as the OD, the astral light to others and the magnetic fluid to yet more. It was a natural composite agent, a fluid force that Eliphas Levi said would receive the vibrations of the will via meditation. It was a force acted upon by the frequency of thought. Levi stated that it was a force that illuminates the mind, vivifies and destroys, separates and coagulates - all depending upon the will of the individual. According to 17th century writer, J. B. van Helmont in his *Hortus Medicine*, it is 'a magical force, sent asleep by sin, is latent in man; it can be awakened by God or by the art of the Cabala.' And what is this force? As Eliphas Levi again tells us in his *History of Magic*:

> 'It has been said that this agent is a light of life by which animated beings are rendered magnetic [electromagnetic energy], electricity being only a transient perturbation. The practice of that marvelous Kabalah reposes entirely in the knowledge and use of this agent. Practical Magic alone opens the secret Temple of Nature to that power of the human will which is ever limited but ever progressive.' *History of Magic,* Eliphas Levi, Weiser, 1999.

And yet, as we saw with Bram Stoker, this invasive dark world of magic was putting a strain on the upright Christian ethics prevalent in the West and many openly fought its influence. In *La Messe Noire* (The Black Mass) from 1924, J. Bricaud we find the following statement:

> 'Today, when our society is invaded by the eroticism of the Middle Ages sorcery, the words Black Mass have last their primitive meaning... The mystic element weakening, sadism and sensualism alone remained, degenerating these last years into vulgar orgy, so-called revival of pagan ceremonies, accompanied by lewd scenes, excited by the rhythm of libidinous poetry and the intoxication of oriental perfumes.'

In short, we are told that the frenzies of the sexual rites associated with the rising of these so-called powerful occult forces were vulgar to the Christian West.

In the *Morning Post* of 16th January,1931, there was an interview with a certain Harry Price, the founder and director of the National Laboratory for Psychical Research, itself connected with Conan Doyle, who stated:

> 'Mr Price spoke from close personal experience of the practices which he described, and among a number of other striking allegations he asserted that black magic, sorcery, and witchcraft are practiced in London of today on a scale and with a freedom undreamed of in the Middle Ages. Professors and leaders of the cults, for the most part foreigners, make use of the same formulae and incantations as the medieval necromancers. The cults are increasing and attracting interest at such a pace that they will soon assume such dimensions as to become a genuine menace to the morals and sanity of the nation… I can safely say that there are more devotees of the Black Arts in London today than ever there were in the Middle Ages.'

We are told that literary groups, such as those of the Bloomsbury Set or Black Mass were full of adherents to the occult, they were also joined by people such as Conan Doyle, Ian Fleming, Bram Stoker and H. G. Wells. Harry Price also informed the *Morning Post* on 19th January, 1931 that the universities of Oxford, Cambridge, and much of scholarly London, were infested with the Black Arts, creating a kind of mass hypnotism. Emerging from these groups we find such people as Aleister Crowley, creating his own occult groups and influencing a great many writers thereafter.

To me there are several points of discussion in this little snapshot of history. Firstly, we see Harry Price pointing out that many of those influencing the minds of British citizens were foreigners and thus we have that spiritual invasion spoken of by Bram Stoker in *Dracula*. Then we have here the birth of subsequent revolutions such as the Sixties and Seventies hippie drug revolutions (for instance Crowley being found on the cover of The Beatles Sergeant Pepper's album). We are shown that sexual license and drug- induced frenzies ("intoxication") are supposedly leading these people on the downward path to the world of Satan. There is nothing new in any

Aleister Crowley The great beast himself.

of this, for it has been repeating for millennia. Freemasonry itself, amongst many others, claims descent, ultimately from Egypt, where drugs were heavily influential in the spiritual and magical life. Initiates were, and still are in some cults, subjected to horrifying trials of darkness, fire, water, and long fasts leading to visions. Should they survive sane then they were accepted into the fold. Hallucination was one of the prime methods in Egyptian theurgy, using opium, datura, henbane, hasheesh, cinnamon and laurel creating vapors, which brought on the frenzy of the prophet.

But, we also see that we have here two distinct opposites and very little balance. On the one side we have thoughtful, intelligent people discovering freedom from a Victorian and religious yoke, like children showing off in front of their friends. On the other side we have the parents - the Christian old school - who are shocked at their youngsters actions and can accept nothing good in what they see.

What is the truth, now, as we stand in the 21st century looking back at these birth pangs of a free society? Well, far be it for me to state what truth is in respect of spirituality - that is the individual's choice and theirs alone. However, I can see, from an historical perspective, that these opposites serve nobody too well, except in raising temperatures. I accept that drug-induced sexual frenzies may well be going over the top and are simply leading the individuals towards a bio-chemical and electromagnetic reaction within the mind – heightening many things! It may also be raising frequencies to levels that do allow a certain lucidity in the mind – creating a free-flow of thought. On the other hand, to stand apart from this with dogmatic eyes and say that it's nonsense, whilst believing that a 33-year-old Jew died on a cross and then got up again 2,000-years ago is also just as improbable to me. Science should be applied to the altered states of mind experienced by millions of people, and it is, but this same science also tells us that walking on water is quite impossible.

It is time to possibly bring all these elements together. To think once again about God, altered states of our own mind and nature itself. To do what our wise men have done in the past and consider possibilities, in as balanced a way as we can.

There do still remain fundamental questions, even for those who have led themselves into a world of delusion and illu-

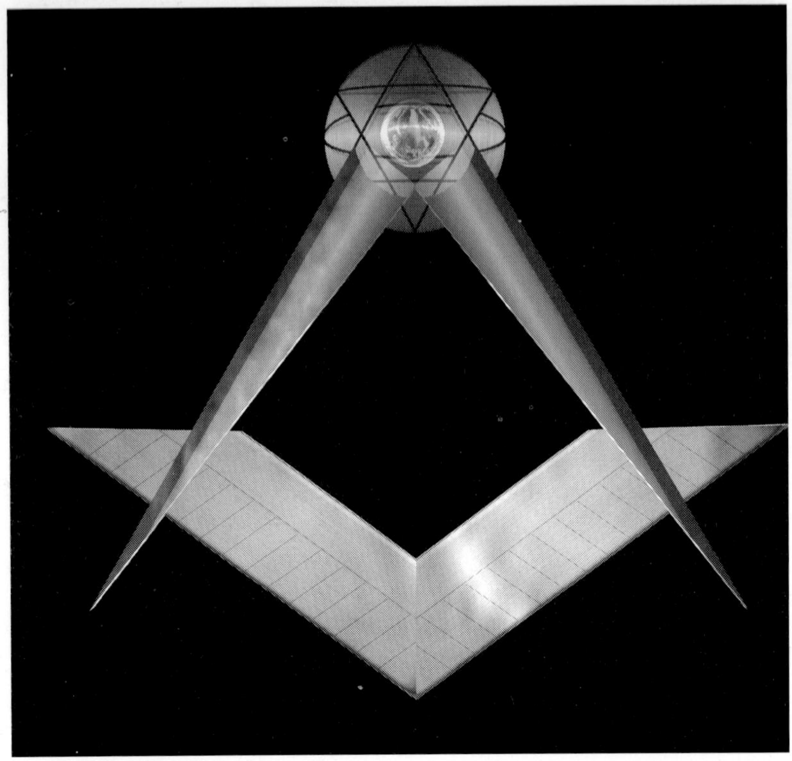

The Masonic symbol points up and down, to the minor and the major.

sion. These questions are as old as man himself (if not older) and we may, or may not, be closer to finding answers.

What is the meaning of existence?

Is there a god? A Great Architect?

Is there a truth, searched for by countless generations and lost in the mists of time?

The drive to find the answer to the ultimate question is not over, but today we have a new science, a new terminology to explain and expound upon the biggest of truths. The answers may not be what we expect. They may not be the gods we have been led to believe in, but they may, very well, answer some of the most profound questions man has ever asked.

The truth of our very existence; the truth about our inner self and the answers to the ultimate question – 'Does god exist?' – may be soon revealed.

John Steinbeck said in *The Log from the Sea of Cortez*, *'Man is related inextricably to all reality, known and unknowable, plankton, a shimmering phospherescence on the sea and the spinning planets and an expanding universe, all bound together by the elastic string of time. It is advisable to look from the tide pool to the stars and then back to the tide pool again.' The Log from the Sea of Cortez.* John Steinbeck, Penguin Classics, 1995.

The universe is an awe-inspiring place, a macrocosmic tidal pool filled with galaxies and yet also quite empty to our perceptions.

Around 10 to 15 billion years ago, existence began and time erupted into a void of nothingness with the comically named Big Bang. The term was given by Fred Hoyle, the controversial astronomer, who paradoxically believed in a totally different concept he called the Steady State Theory, whereby the universe gradually emerges, rather than in one incredible explosion. Today, scientists have all but proven the big bang theory with measurements of red and blue shift, the coming towards and going away noise seen in the red and blue extremes of the light spectrum. In addition to this at the end of the last century scientists discovered background radiation signatures from the very first cosmic moments of the big bang.

In these early moments of a new existence the mathematical equations of all things were being worked out from the initial chaos. Mathematical laws underpin the fabric of the universe, not just atoms, but people, stars and galaxies. Modern mathematicians are proving theories espoused by our Gnostic and esoteric ancestors – that we are related, via geometry, to the very universe, that we cannot be separated from it, for we are part of it, alive and conscious of ourself.

Inside every atom there are beautiful mathematical forces binding them together and these bind everything else – our skin, the land, the planets and gravity itself.

Inside every atom there is also a huge space – an empty void, little understood by science. Not surprisingly the same thing occurs in the vastness of space. We term this void 'dark matter' because we do not understand it. It is like the mind, what we see is consciousness – the part of our mind we are aware of. Yet, also within our mind is dark matter we call the unconscious world. We are only aware of this world in our dreams or in conscious lucid dreaming. We need to place different filters on the lenses of our telescopes to realize that there is much more to the Universe than we can see with our eyes. In fact, we have found a great many ways of altering our perception of it, just as we have discovered many ways of altering our state of consciousness to peer into the dark matter of the mind.

The average concentration of atoms in the universe is .2 atoms per cubic meter. This is what we see, four percent of what is actually in existence. In fact most of the material in the universe emits no light, no infra-red heat, no radio waves or any other kind of radiation and so it is consequently almost impossible to detect. We have to dream of its existence. We have to infer its properties from what we know. How true this is of our own unconscious self and if consciousness is but four percent of our mind that we can see then how much more is there to know?

Scientists have found almost weightless and electrically neutral particles called neutrinos. These are exotic particles that go right through the earth itself. In truth, they are like the neurons firing in our brains – the thought particles. Incredibly, just as the neutrino is electrically neutral, we too have to be in a neutral state to understand and access our unconscious world. We have to be neither awake, nor asleep.

If a correlation were drawn between ourselves and the greater universe – then the galaxies of light would be the conscious world and dark matter would be the unconscious.

We are in a remarkable likeness to the universe – to what some would call God.

Clement of Alexandria said:

> *"For the image of God is His Word, the genuine son of mind, the divine word, the archetypal light of light, the image of the word is the true man." Exhortation to the Greeks 10.*

This word is a vibration from the very heart of the creation, from the heart of dark matter – it is a mathematical equation fostering life, light and mind and it surges through our veins even now. And, I believe, when it becomes conscious, as in the case of human beings, and recognizes itself as such, something very special happens...

And as we shall see, the form of the crystal, configured just like the universe and indeed our own mind, is also mainly empty space. It is in this space that scientists store and harness vast amounts of information – in the dark matter of the crystal.

St Augustine said *"The universe was brought into being in a less than fully formed state, but was gifted to transform itself from unformed matter into a truly marvelous array of structure and life forms." De Genesi ad Litteram*, St. Augustine

That gifting, spoken of by St Augustine sixteen-hundred years ago is now known by scientists as a mathematical equation, but this does not reveal a purpose – a 'why', instead it only reveals how it was formed. The answer to why may well be found within the mind of what we can only call god.

A series of special numbers now exist which explain how all things work, from the atom to the largest sun. Gravity, electromagnetism, time, light and all-manner of phenomena emerged with interlinked and intertwined mathematical strands that unite all things to each other. What was created, was a wonderful crystal-like structure often termed the Matrix.

> *'We must assume behind this force the existence of a conscious and intelligent mind. This mind is the matrix of all matter.'* A saying attributed to Max Planck.

As humans, we are poised at the very center of this incredible force. It would take as many humans to make up the mass of our Sun as there are atoms within each one of us. The sun is a billion meters in diameter and a molecule is a billionth of a meter. We are perfectly situated in between. This is perfection in a mathematically balanced nature and yet we are unaware of our special position.

Our size and our position in the solar system is crucial for life to exist as it does. It is the nature of number that allows this wonder - an equation first formed in the original moments - according to Max Plank, mind of the big bang.

Molecules, living cells and minerals are all formed by atoms combining together in special mixes to create different substances. All are atoms, all are particles, all have sub-nuclear particles, and the galaxies themselves are held in position by these sub-nuclear particles, and of course those mathematical ratios. What scientists do not yet know are the ultimate questions for them - What is the synthesis between the cosmos and the quantum world? What is the thread that links the quantum to the cosmos?

It is because of division in language and perception that this answer cannot be found. I believe we will discover this secret wave-like thread and find that if we pull upon it, we shall unravel the mysteries of the universe.

Crystal

The word crystal is derived over time from several languages, including Greek and Latin, and means variously ice or hard solid surface. The word itself does not sum up the beautiful nature of the structure of crystal - nor the vast untapped depths of its inner spaces - the void within. Yet within the mathematical equations and the wonder of the crystalline form can be found great depth.

The universe is often said to be of crystalline form -- a series of strings and lattices - a matrix of creation of platonic forms built one upon the other; from the very particle in the atom to the solar systems within the galaxy. From the vast universe and down to the formations of galaxies and even further into our very DNA, the forms and structures of the crystal can be found.

When water turns to ice we see beautiful crystal forms appear - snow flakes and ice crystals. Humans themselves are composed of mainly water and so we are fluid crystal forms ourselves. Even our society forms in crystalline shapes as we merge together as if drops within the ocean of humanity. But, we are also whole people within a greater whole itself.

Water is a fluid substance, a cleansing substance. It has been seen across time as a sacred domain - a world linked inextri-

All things are connected, did our ancestors truly believe this?

cably to the unconscious self. It mirrors the vibrations of the world and even the solar and lunar system around it. The molecular structure of water is even actually affected by crystals. The sea itself moves in wave-like form in accordance with the gravitational push and pull of the moon – it is part of a greater whole pulled by the wave-like force of gravity. If the seas and oceans are affected in this way, then we too are part of the greater whole and we too are affected by the same influences. These influences come in the form of waves, whether gravity, energy or light – whether from the universe, our earth or even crystals.

To be alive, water needs vibration – a waveform. All life needs a waveform, the energy spark created at the very beginning. Existence is in fact vibration – like a word spoken and given life.

> *"In the beginning was the word, and the word was with god, and the word was god."* Genesis

Dr Masaru Emoto is now infamous for having taken a range of remarkable photographs of water crystals forming and showing how human emotions actually affected the beauty of the formation. The question is, how is this possible? Emoto puts this down to the wave form – vibration from our own thoughts.

The whole universe is like this – in a state of vibration – whether a piece of wood or a tectonic plate; all things vibrate. And crystals too sing to the harmony of vibration.

Quartz crystal begins its life deep within the earth from hot vapour, which is a supersaturated solution of silicon dioxide. As it cools a unit cell of quartz forms around a nucleating site in the same way that an oyster forms. It is a matrix created around a seed point. The forming atoms and bonding are laid down where there is most energy – the molecules adhering to the base silicon matrix. Made up as a tetrahedron-shaped molecule it is now composed of four atoms of oxygen with one silicon atom suspended within. This primary cell unit now attracts other silicon dioxide molecules and over time trillions of these cells link together in a *spiralling motion*, layer upon layer until the crystal is made.

The crystal is a known quantum converter that is able to transmit energy in a magnified state and this energy can easily be absorbed or received by biological matter – such as the

Does the crystal form hold clues to the higher nature of man?

human body. The crystal is formed via a wave-like spiralling motion and is a known quantum converter transmitting energy-information at a magnified rate.

Stimulating a crystal makes it vibrate or "sing." These vibrations make waves, which human receptors pick up and convert back to binary information. This means that vibratory information or energy of different frequencies can be stored inside the empty space like memory. This is no different to what we shall see with dark matter, the space within the atom and of course the unconscious world of the mind. This is also why scientists today use crystal within the heart of computers.

These crystals do much more though - they also amplify the energy like Temples magnifying sound. Dark Matter in our universe does exactly the same thing. We can see distant galaxies because dark matter magnifies their existence - bringing the light into our consciousness. In sleep, the dark matter of our mind or our unconscious world, mirrors this process and highlights to us issues about our own self that our conscious world needs to work upon.

Crystals and their prism structures can be found at every level of existence. From the S-Matrix of the subatomic domain to the nature of molecules, from crystal-like gravity fields and even magnetism - the crystal structure is all permeating.

By moving crystals, applying pressure or other stimuli, such as touch, they can be forced to offer up their locked-in information energy - such as that of the holographic universe or matrix to which all things are connected, including the wave-particles within the crystal. The same is also true of our unconscious world, which reacts according to psychological stimuli. Is this also true of the dark matter of the universe itself? Can we stimulate the mind of the universe to offer up its inner most secrets?

Within the crystal structure, whether quartz, magnetite, the brain or the universe as a whole, there is a marvelous truth embedded and awaiting release.

Our ancestors built around the globe a huge array of sacred temples and monuments. Many of these encompass the archetypal forms seen in nature; others mirror the patterns and movements of the planets; others still are the great *axis mundi* - the gateway to heaven or illumination. However, in a lot of these locations we also find the use of granite, which is mostly quartz crystal. The King's Chamber in the Great Pyramid, for instance, is encased in granite and Jacob's ladder to the seven levels of heaven was only envisaged once Jacob laid his head upon a granite stone slab.

For centuries, if not thousands of years, people have recognized something special in crystals. They have been used for physical and spiritual healing and people feel a close affinity to them and are drawn to them for some peculiar and untold reason. They resonate or vibrate at specific frequencies, which, if we were able, we would hear as beautiful harmonic music. This is the music of the universe.

Quartz crystal resonates at a frequency that is perfectly in-tune with the frequency of the human mind when about to enter an altered state of consciousness – it is on the point of sleep, before we enter our unconscious world. That is, the very substance found beneath Jacob's head and encasing the King's Chamber actually resonates at that special frequency utilized by shaman throughout time to connect with the gods.

The world of the unconscious is the world not closed to the

There may be as much truth found in the minor as there is in the major.

nature of the cosmos as our conscious mind often is. The unconscious world is free to think, not cluttered by the world we have created.

There is more to the tale, for along with every wave or resonance there is the particle. The wave and particle are not divided, only we do this. They are instead the wave-particle united as one. So, what is a particle? It is the messenger carried along the energy wave.

Light particles travel to our eye along light waves and in the same way thought particles travel along thought waves within our mind. This is the world of quantum physics - the world of the sub-atomic. Everything is made of atoms and within every atom are particles - messengers carrying information via resonance. It is like a mini world of mandalas.

Mandalas are our image of the structure of all and oneness. They are visualized crystals building one layer upon another into a beautiful shape. A mandala is a drawing or structure used by adepts in the East to visualize existence itself and, in so doing, they are visualizing something that cannot be seen by the human eye. Instead they are utilizing the third eye - the intuitive state which works best when the mind resonates at the same frequency as quartz crystal and indeed the Earth itself. This is the point of connection between man and nature - our true state of knowing. And this is the point of contact Paracelsus and others throughout this book have come to in their own way.

Via a new science known as quantum entanglement, scientists have proven that particles of thought can, indeed, entangle with another persons thought particles. This was much more effective when two participating individuals were emotionally attached and less effective when they did not know each other. This is a kind of extra-sensory perception and it is a natural state that we have forgotten how to use or hear - at least forgotten in our conscious realm.

The world is full of too many perception grabbing things - clutter for the conscious mind - that we no longer even realize that there is indeed more depth to our state of being. By following what our alchemical and Gnostic friends of the past told us, we can reduce this clutter and burn it off, thus revealing a world below that has long since been forgotten.

Scientists at the Stanford University of Education said *'A pair of quantum systems in an entangled state can be used as a quantum information channel to perform computational and cryptographic tasks that are impossible for classical systems.'* http://plato.stanford.edu/entries/qt-entangle/. It is a method of information exchange that is non-classical; that is, not as we generally understand.

The question now is, if we can entangle with the particles of thought of another person, then can we entangle with the particles within the great crystal universe itself?

The pineal organ is one of the outgrowths of the pineal apparatus. In aquatic and gill-breathing creatures, it can form a photosensitive eye-like structure which is involved in the diurnal rhythm of color change. In ancient reptiles, it formed a separate, or third, eye on top of the head. It persists in higher vertebrates and may function as an endocrine gland, internally secreting into the blood and affecting distant parts of the body. The pineal gland exerts some chemical reactions, which are not fully understood. Autopsies on mediums and spiritually inclined people have revealed larger pineal glands that contain a clear fluid called serotonin, which in turn makes melatonin. Serotonin, when depleted by amphetamines, causes mild psychedelic effects. Strangely, it is also thought to influence our rhythms of activity. The pineal gland is associated with color recognition, and reptiles can change the colour of this third eye. It is also associated with measuring the length of the day and keeping track of the seasons. It is sensitive to the rhythms and cycles of nature and is responsible for transferring that information to us – it is the connection point to nature itself, talking to us and passing on information.

Many animals have a variety of senses, which we are yet to understand, such as the ability to emit small electrical discharges, underwater vibrations, infrasound and ultrasound. Some birds can detect polarized light, which helps them to see the fingerprint of their prey as it leaves a pattern across the ground. Snakes can see and produce images in infra-red radiation. Can man use more senses than we know? Should we believe that the dowser's skill is simply that they are more acutely in touch with their senses?

The term to be 'mesmerised' comes from the Austrian physician Franz Anton Mesmer (1734-1815) who believed the human nervous system to be magnetised. He coined the phrase 'animal magnetism' and claimed that magnetism from the planets had actually caused healing at one church in

Austria. He developed a therapeutic regime, which incorporated iron magnets, magnetite and the laying on of hands. Mesmer built up a large following, many of whom claimed to have been healed by his 'animal magnetism'. The modern-day term for mesmerism is hypnotism and it is at this point - the hypnotic state - that our mind resonates at that special quartz frequency.

Researchers have found that magnetite actually clusters around the pineal gland within our brain and magnetite itself is a wonderful crystal linking our intuitive natural state with the natural world around us. Our consciousness has divided us from the true abilities of our own mind.

So, through the electromagnetic connection within our mind, via the magnetite and pineal system, we can actually intuitively understand directional information. We can know where we are and which way we need to go because the wave carrier of electromagnetism carries the information messengers of particles. Our ancestors also told us that we can understand much more - that we can be one with the word - with god.

If we therefore entangle with particles, not just those of other humans with whom we feel an emotional connection, but with nature - especially if we have an emotional connection to nature - then we can form as one mind with nature itself - the mind of god.

Our ancestors used to thank the earth - the mother - for the produce, for the animals and plants, for the water. They used to thank the solar god in the sky for the light and heat. They respected themselves, because they were part of the whole. Today we disrespect nature and rape her without thanks and without thought. What message are we sending to our selves?

People like Masaru Emoto and the science of quantum physics reveals the mind of god - the mind of the oneness to us all. We can see a consciousness actually at work like never before. All we have to do is join the dots and we see the bigger picture. What do quantum scientists say?

James Gardner is a complexity theorist and peer reviewed scientific writer whose biocosm theory proposes that the appearance of life in the universe is no accident or chance event. Rather, he views life as an expression of a great cosmic intelligence, hardwired into a timeless, dynamic cycle of creation, evolution, and renewal. The ultimate purpose of highly evolved life, Gardner argues, is ultimately to infuse the entire universe with intelligence, eventually creating a single, vast, cosmic life form.

The universe is intelligent at the sub-atomic level and acts like a DNA feedback loop. DNA sends out purposeful signals in order to grow. Then it stops and waits for a signal to come back before proceeding. In this way, life is formed in perfect continuity with its surroundings and according to an incredible mathematically complex design. The universe seems to be doing exactly the same thing at the sub-atomic and quantum level.

The universe is a vast vibrating crystal form no different to our own brain. It is linked mathematically and via quantum mechanics to the wave-particle of thought – in fact, the evidence is now revealing that every facet of the universe is part of a Grand Mind.

Our problem is that we have divided nature into compartments and no longer see the whole. We have named everything and in so doing we have reduced them down to constituent parts. We have separated them from one another and this is not reality, but our own created reality. The truth of the existence of all things will and can only be found in realising the whole and not the parts. As John Ciardi said

> *'Who could believe an ant in theory? A giraffe in blueprint? Ten thousand doctors of what's possible could reason half the jungle out of being.'* http://www.encyclopedia.com/doc/1G1-14960792.html

Sir Isaac Newton used a crystal to separate light into the spectrum. He divided the wave and particle stream so that what he saw was the divided parts. He then used another crystal to form them back together again. When all these colors are formed back as one, the result is pure white light. Purity is found in the whole, undivided nature.

Nature without the supposed, conscious self-awareness of man and his inherent free-will does not name and divide. Instead, it forms balance when left alone. It comes back together in accordance with the natural laws of mathematics in-built into all things. By dividing nature, we upset the mathematical purposefulness of it, we divide more than just our own minds, we divide ourselves from it. When a crystal is sliced in half and then placed side by side, the two divided parts form back together again, in perfection. It is the law. We have forgotten this intuitive process, we are divided by our own free will from the pure white light.

There is a deeper concept here and one that reveals the mind of the Great Architect himself.

Quantum physics states that when we observe a particle, we can cause an affect by our own free will. Mathematical equations suggest to us what the majority of particles will do, but every now and then one or another particle will "decide" to do something different. This is a kind of chaos theory, as if by naming it we can understand it. The truth is that scientists do not understand the complexity of it all.

In the same way, we can mathematically predict what a group of humans will do. But, every now and then one of them will do something different, because of its free will and own complexities. How is it that we can say the free will of the human is the explanation for this mathematical conundrum and yet accuse the particle of chaos?

The truth is that the particle is acting according to some kind of free will and so, what has been stated for thousands of years and is now coming into scientific realization, is the fact that there is a greater mind at work. That mind is seen in the glorious mathematics derived from the early stages of the big bang itself and so that mind is the mind of the creator. It is ultimate free will.

This is the thread between the cosmos and the quantum world. This is the unifying concept – the connection missed by division between right and left hemispheres. It is mind, awareness, conscious-minded nature at the heart of it all, born from, of and giving birth to the big bang itself.

That mind is the universal quantum crystal prism. We can peer into that crystal and see the beautiful colors of the rainbow – but one thing is sure – we will also see our selves.

It is not dark matter – it is the quantum mind of god.

Chapter 9

A Message from the Past

We have seen now, how wise men of the real world have picked up on sources of wisdom, and run amok with it in literature and elsewhere. We have seen how their ideas were not so new, but were, in fact, based upon much more ancient concepts, and yet we have also seen how the knowledge of science today is forcing a rethink back yet again to these ancient concepts. I wish to write the final chapter of this book now with a fable – a story of a man who may have been real, but who has fallen into the world of folklore, myth and legend, but with an angle that drives home for me the whole purpose of gaining knowledge and becoming wise – Nature herself.

Almost everybody in the UK, if not the Western world, will know of the tale of King Canute and how he tried to turn back the sea, but is everybody aware of the esoteric teaching behind this remarkable story?

The time is the 11th century and the Viking Canute (Knut) is

Cnut or Canute is the one on the bottom right, with one hand on his sword for strength and one on the cross of Christ. This depiction reveals a perfect balance of male and female and indeed form and structure.

King of Demark, Norway and England. He was a very real King and his tomb can, to this day, be seen in Winchester, England.

But, as with most monarchs and people in power, there erupts around them all manner of weird and wonderful folk-tales. Many are based upon the art-form of propaganda but many are also based upon the sacred teachings of esoteric societies. In this instance we have a little of both, as the tale erupted well after the death of the King, and so was therefore Christian and monarchist propaganda – and yet it was released by brothers who knew the esoteric truths.

The story goes that the courtiers of King Canute were so overwhelmed with his leadership qualities, that they constantly adored him and praised his every move. One day Canute was walking by the sea with his courtiers praising him as usual. He eventually grew weary of this praise and decided he would teach them all a lesson and said:

'So you say I am the greatest man in the world?'

To which they replied:

'O King, there has never been anyone as mighty as you.'

'And you say all things obey my word?'

'Yes my lord, all things bow before you.'

'In that case bring me my chair and we will go down to the water.'

Although the courtiers were puzzled, they did as they were told and the King's chair was placed close by the sea.

'Very well Sea, I command you to come no further.' said the King.

Of course they all waited and as we all know the sea refused to listen to the commands of the King. Finally, he said:

'Let it be known to all inhabitants of the world that the power of kings is empty, and no one is worthy of the name king except Him, whose will is obeyed by Heaven, earth and sea.'

We do know that the real King Canute was a religious man, with many non-Christian Viking styled followers who had

Could Canute hold back the waters?

followed him to England and so he ruled a religiously divided nation. It seems he respected the Ch ristian Church and spent a lot of time, and energy, rebuilding the various churches and monasteries, in this way showing his allegiance to the power of the Church and according to some[1] had early but distinctly Masonic tendencies – using the buildings as symbols of the Great Architect's power. In this fable, however, we may have a hint of Christian propaganda revealing that the King himself is subject to the power of God (and therefore the Pope) in the form of the waves. As this story is obviously a fable and in all likelihood not a true literal account, then we do have to find the reason for it and as with many things there are many answers.

The most often used explanation for this tale, is that it proves that no man is above the law of nature, created by God, and this is very true, however, there is depth here that is taught in several esoteric schools, and never passed on to the uninitiated. I believe it is time for the true depth of this teaching to surface.

To understand exactly what we are talking about here, we

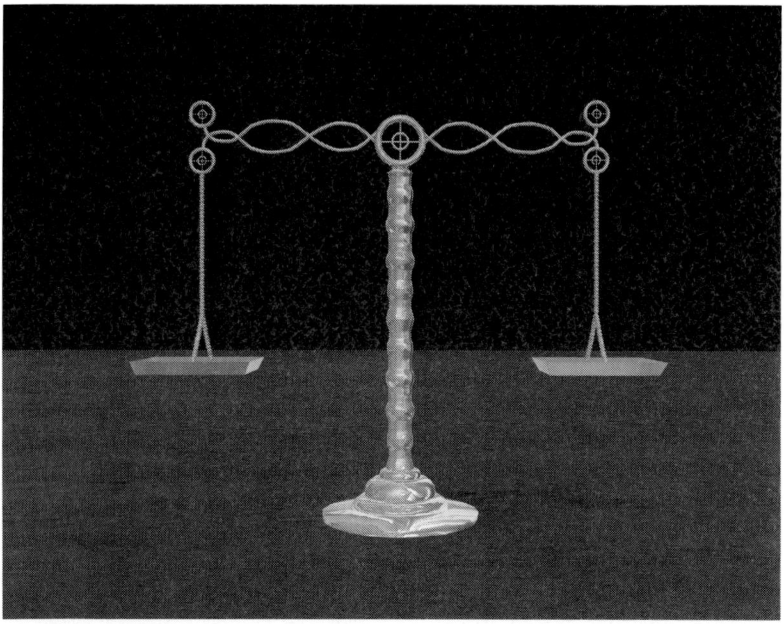

Conclusion Balance
In all things, we must maintain balance, whether between strength and compassion or positive and negative.

will have to alter our perceptions slightly. Firstly, we need to understand that the King in the story could have been any King. It simply uses him as the figurehead, the role. The King is in the role of our consciousness and indeed he is the head of the State and our own head. This King is our male-dominated consciousness that is so constantly spoken about. We build up our own self-worth with our own thoughts – here portrayed as courtiers – the courtiers of the mind. In our conscious state we believe that we are in charge, that we control our actions, that we can do anything. This is not necessarily a bad thing, but it can become so if it is out of balance with nature itself.

Inside all of us, the power of nature surges, like the sea, and if we believe that we can control or turn back this powerful tide, then we are indeed fools and not Kings. As an example, I will create a fictional role. Let us say that my wife has a deep, natural urge to nurture and care for young. She is attracted to puppies' eyes and baby seals, as we all are to some extent. This is a natural urge and a good one. If this urge gets out of control, or out of balance, then we will end up with a houseful of children and baby animals, but she curbs the desire and balances it out with her conscious knowledge. However, if she denies the power of the urge, the natural urge that sources through her very veins, then she will be a mental and physical wreck, because the natural urges will never cease and allow her a moment's emotional rest. She will be denying an essence that is from within the heart of the very universe – the essence of life and life-creation.

No man or woman on this planet can deny the natural urges that are within us, creating desires, loves, hunger and all manner of emotions that, when out of balance, simply form an unnatural state and division and duality. When Arthur and Guinevere were split apart, the land became infertile. When Solomon and Sheba were parted, Israel divided; and Robin Hood was nothing without Marion. We must be in union inside our minds with the natural world, with our natural state. We cannot fight it, but we must live with it in balance and harmony.

King Canute as our male conscious self, was simply balancing the worldly thoughts of power that we all have, with the knowledge of the power of nature to which we are all subject. In this way, when we too believe that we can fight our natural urges, then we need to think again and understand nature for what it truly is. These urges are not those bastardised forms that excuse a man of rape, no, these are pure and wholesome. They can be easily recognised because they will be beautifully creative moments and will be in perfect balance with that wee-small-voice we know as intuition.

The outer shell we believe to be "ourselves" is in truth the creation of others, of time and our own experiences. The real you or I lies at the very centre of our being and it is in perfect connection to the universe. The problem is that because of a lifetime of "input" we have lost the ability to see or hear it.

King Canute was indeed a wise King (or at least the people who wrote the tale), a clever consciousness, as he knew he was only powerful because he understood nature and his place in it. His courtiers – the "input" – were fools, who did not.

Time and tide, wait for no man.

Notes

[1] *Arcane Schools* by John Yarker www.masonicworld.com/education/files/artjuno02/YARKERAS4.htm

Bibliography

Ashe, Geoffrey, *The Quest for Arthur's Britain*, Paladin, 1971, London
Baigent, Leigh, *The Elixir and the Stone*, Viking, 1997. London
Baigent, Leigh, Lincoln, *The Holy Blood and the Holy Grail*, Jonathan Cape, 1982. London
Baigent, Leigh, Lincoln, *The Messianic Legacy*, Arrow, 1996. London
Baigent, Michael, Leigh, Richard, *The Temple and the Lodge*, Arrow, 1998. London
Balfour, Mark, *The Sign of the Serpent*, Prism, 1990. London
Barber, Malcolm, *The Trial of the Templars*, Cambridge University Press, 1978. Cambridge.
Barrett, David V., *Sects, Cults and Alternative Religions*, Blandford, 1996. London
Barrow, John D., *Theories of Everything*, Virgin. 1990. London
Bayley, H., *The Lost Language of Symbolism*, Bracken Books, 1996. London
Beatty, Longfield, *The Garden of the Golden Flower*, Senate, 1996. London
Begg, E. & Begg. D., *In Search of the Holy Grail and the Precious Blood*, Thorsons, 1985. London
Blaire, Lawrence, *Rhythms of Vision*, Warner Books, New York, 1975.
Blavatsky, H.P., *Theosophical Glossary*, R. A. Kessinger Publishing Ltd, 1918. MT
Borchant, Bruno, *Mysticism*, Weisner, 1994. Colorado
Bouquet A.C., *Comparative Religion*, Pelican, 1942. London
Bryant, N., *The High Book of the Grail*, D S Brewer, 1985. Cambridge
Bryden, R., *Rosslyn – a History of the Guilds, the Masons and the Rosy Cross*, Rosslyn Chapel Trust, 1994. Edinburgh
Budge, E. A. Wallis, *An Egyptian Hieroglyphic Dictionary Volume 1*, Dover Publications, 1978. Dover
Butcher, William, *Jules Verne: The Definitive Biography*, Thunders Mouth Press, New York, 2006
Butler, E.M., *The Myth of the Magus*, CUP. 1948, Cambridge
Callahan, Philip, S., *Paramagnetism: Rediscovering Nature's Secret Force of Growth*, Acres, USA 1995.
Callahan, Philip, S., *Ancient Mysteries Modern Visions: The Magnetic Life of Agriculture*, Acres, USA, 2001.
Callahan, Philip, S., *Nature's Silent Music*, Acres, USA, 1992
Campbell, Joseph, *Transformations of Myth Through Time*, Harper and Row, 1990. London
Carr-Gomm, Sarah, *Dictionary of Symbols in Art*, Duncan Baird Publishers, 1995. Winchester.
Cavendish, Richard, *Mythology*, Tiger, 1998. London

Carpenter, Edward, *Pagan and Christian Creeds: Their Origin and Meaning*, Allen and Unwin Ltd, 1920. London
Clarke, Hyde and Wake, C. Staniland, *Serpent and Siva Worship,* R. A. Kessinger Publishing Ltd, 1877. London
Cooper, J.C., *An Illustrated Encyclopaedia of Traditional Symbols,* Thames and Hudson, 1978. London
Currer-Briggs, N., *The Shroud and the Grail; a modern quest for the true grail*, St Martins Press. New York
Davidson, H. R. Ellis, *Myths and Symbols of Pagan Europe*, Syracuse University Press. Syracuse
Davidson, John, *The Secret of the Creative Vacuum,* The C. W. Daniel Company Ltd, 1989. MA
De Martino, Ernesto, *Primitive Magic,* Prism Unity, 1972. Bridport
Dodd, C.H., *Historical Tradition of the Fourth Gospel,* Cambridge University Press. Cambridge.
Duckett, Shipley, Eleanor, *The Gateway to the Middle Ages, Monasticism,* Ann Arbor Paperbacks - the University of Michigan Press, 1961. Michigan
Eliade, Mircea, *Shamanism: Archaic Techniques of Ecstasy*, Princeton University Press. 1951, Princeton.
Epstein, Perle, *Kabbalah: The Way of the Jewish Mystic,* Shambhala Classics, 2001. Chodron, Pema
Evans, Lorraine, *Kingdom of the Ark*, Simon and Schuster, 2000. London
Evans, A. B. (1988). *Jules Verne rediscovered: Didacticism and the scientific novel*. Westport, CT: Greenwood Press.
Fedder, Kenneth L., Park, Michael Alan, *Human Antiquity: An Introduction to Physical Anthropology and Archaeology,* Mayfield Publishing Company, 1993. Caliufornia
Fontana, David, *The Secret Language of Symbols,* Piatkus, 1997. London
Fortune, Dion, *The Mystical Qabalah,* Weiser Books, 2000. New York
Foss, Michael, *People of the First Crusade,* Michael O'Mara Books, 1997. London
Frazer, Sir James, *The Golden Bough*, Wordsworth, 1993. London
Freke, Timothy, Gandy, Peter, *Jesus and the Goddess*, Thorsons, 2001. London
Gallagher, E. J. (1980). *Jules Verne: A primary and secondary bibliography*. Boston: MA, G. K. Hall & Co.
Gardiner, Samnuel R., *History of England,* Longmans, Green and Co., 1904. London
Gascoigne, Bamber, *The Christians*, Jonathan Cape, 1977. London
Gerber, Richard, *Vibrational Medicine,* Bear & Company, 2001. Santa Fe
Gilbert, Adrian, *Magi*, Bloomsbury, 1996. London
Goldberg, Carl, *Speaking With The Devil*, Viking, 1996. London

Gould, Charles: *Mythical Monsters*, Senate, 1995. London
Graves, Robert, *The Greek Myths: 2*, Pelican, 1964. London
Guenther, Johannes Von, *Cagliostro*, William Heinemann, 1928. London
Hagger, Nicholas, *The Fire and the Stones*, Element, 1991. London
Hancock, Graham, *The Sign and the Seal*, Arrow, 2001. London
Halifax, Joan, *Shaman: the Wounded Healer*, Crossroad, Thames and Hudson. London
Harrington, E., *The Meaning of English Place Names*, The Black Staff Press. 1954. Belfast
Hedsel, Mark, *The Zelator*, Century, 1998. London
Howard, M., *The Occult Conspiracy*, Hutchinson. 1989. Rochester
James, E.O., *The Ancient Gods*, Weidenfeld and Nicolson, 1962. London
Jennings, Hargrave, *Ophiolatreia*. Kessinger Publishing. Year unknown. London
Johnson, Buffie, *Lady of the Beast: the Goddess and Her Sacred Animals*, Harper and Row, 1988. San Fransisco.
Jones, Alison, *Dictionary of World Folklore*, Larousse, 1995. New York
Josephus, *Antiquities*, Indypublish.com
Kauffeld, Carl, *Snakes: The Keeper and the Kept*, Doubleday and Co., 1969. London
Kendrick, T. D., *The Druids*, Methuen and Co., 1927. London
King, Serge Kahili, *Instant Healing: Mastering the Way of the Hawaiian Shaman Using Words, Images, Touch, and Energy*, Renaissance Books, 2000
Knight, Christopher, Lomas, Robert, *The Second Messiah*, Arrow, 1997. London
Laidler, Keith, *The Head of God*, Orion, 1999. London
Laidler, Keith, *The Divine Deception*, Headline, 2000. London
Lamy, Michel, *The Secret Message of Jules Verne: Decoding His Masonic, Rosicrucian, and Occult Writings*, Destiny Books, 2007
Lapatin, Kenneth, *Mysteries of the Snake Goddess*, Houghton Mifflin Company, 2002. London
Le Goff, Jacques, *The Medieval World*, Parkgate Books, 1997. London
Levi, Eliphas, *Transcendental Magic*, Tiger Books, 1995. Twickenham
Lincoln, Henry, *Key to the Sacred Pattern*, The Windrush Press, 1997. Gloucestershire
Loye, David, *An Arrow Through Chaos: how we see into the future*, Inner Traditions International, 1983. Santa Fe
Lynch, L. (1992). *Jules Verne*. New York: Twayne Publishers.
MacCana, Proinsias, *Celtic Mythology*, Hamlyn. 1970. New York
Mack, B.L., *The Lost Gospel*, Element, 1993. London
Martin, A. (1990). *The mask of the prophet: The extraordinary fictions of Jules Verne*. New York: Oxford University Press.
Matthews, John, *Sources of the Grail*, Floris Books, 1996. London
Morton, Chris, and Thomas, Ceri louise, *The Mystery of the Crystal Skulls*, Element, 2003. London

Muggeridge, Malcolm, *Jesus,* Collins, 1975. London
Oliver, George, *Signs and Symbols,* Macoy Publishing. 1906. New York
Oliver, Rev. George, *The History of Initiation,* R. A. Kessinger Publishing Co, 1841. London
O'Neill, John, *Nights of the Gods*, publisher unknown.
Orwell, George, *Wells, Hitler and the World State*,First published: *Horizon*. London. 1941
Pagels, E., *The Gnostic Gospels,* Weidenfeld and Nicolson. 1980. London
Paterson Smyth, J. *How We Got our Bible*, Sampson Low. 1895. London
Piggot, Stuart, *The Druids,* Thames and Hudson. 1985. London
Pike, Albert, *The Morals and Dogma of Scottish Rite Freemasonry*, L.H. Jenkins, 1928. London
Plichta, Peter, *God's Secret Formula,* Element, 1997. London
Powell, T.G.E., *The Celts,* Thames and Hudson. 1989. London
Rabten, Geshe, *Echoes of Voidness*, Wisdom Publications, 1983. London
Radin, Dean, *The Conscious Universe,* Harper Collins, 1997. London
Ravenscroft, Trevor (1982). *The occult power behind the spear which pierced the side of Christ*. Red Wheel, p.165.
Read, Piers Paul, *The Templars,* Phoenix, 1999. London
Reid, Howard, *Arthur - The Dragon King,* Headline, 2001. London
Reid, Howard, *In Search of the Immortals: Mummies, Death and the Afterlife,* Headline, 1999. London
Roberts, Alison, *Hathor Rising: The Serpent Power of Ancient Egypt,* Northgate, 1995. London
Roberts, J.M., *The Mythology of the Secret Societies, Secker and Warburg, 1972, London*
Roberts, J.M. Esq,. *Antiquity Unveiled*, Health Research, 1970. New York
Robertson, J. M., *Pagan Christs,* Watts, 1903. London
Rolleston, T. W., *Myths and Legends of the Celtic Race,* Mystic P, 1986. London
Russell, Peter, *The Brain Book,* Routledge, 1980. London
Scholem, Gershom G., *On the Kabbalah and It's Symbolism*, Routledge & Kegan, London, 1965.
Schonfield, Hugh, *Essene Odyssey,* Element, 1984. London
Schonfield, Hugh, *The Passover Plot,* Hutchinson, 1965. London
Schwartz, Gary, Russek, Linda, *The Living Energy Universe*, Hampton Roads Publishing, 1999. London
Scott, Ernest, *The People of the Secret,* The Octagon Press, 1983. London
Seligmann, Kurt, *The History of Magic,* Quality Paperback Book Club, New York, 1997.

Signs, Symbols and Ciphers, New Horizons. 1989. London
Sharper Knowlson, T., *The Origins of Popular Superstitions and Customs*, Senate, 1994. London
Smith, M., *The Secret Gospel,* Victor Gollancz. 1999. London
Spence, Lewis, *Introduction to Mythology,* Senate, 1994. London
Spence, Lewis, *Myths and Legends of Egypt,* George Harrap and Sons, 1915. London
Talbot, Michael, *The Holographic Universe,* Harper Collins, 1991/1996.London
Thiering, Barbara, *Jesus The Man,* Doubleday, 1992. London
Thiering, Barbara, *Jesus of the Apocalypse,* Doubleday, 1996. London
Tull, George F., *Traces of the Templars,* The Kings England Press, 2000. London
Villars, de, Abbe N. de Montfaucon, *Comte de Gabalis: discourses on the Secret Sciences and Mysteries in accordnace with the principles of the Ancient Magi and the Wisdom of the Kabalistic Philosophers,* 17th century. Kessinger Publishing. London
Waite, Arthur Edward, *The Hidden Church of the Holy Grail,* Fredonia Books, Amsterdam, 2002.
Wake, C. Staniland, *The Origin of Serpent Worship,* R. A. Kessinger Publishing Ltd, 1877. London
Wallace-Murphy, Hopkins, *Rosslyn,* Element, 2000. London
Watson, Lyall, *Dark Nature,* Harper Collins, 1995. London
Weber, Renee, *Dialogues with Scientists and Sages: Search for Unity in Science and Mysticism,* Arkana, 1990. London
Wells, H. G. *The Open Conspiracy and Other Writings,* London, Waterlow and Sons, 1933.
Wilson, Colin, *Beyond the Occult,* Caxton Editions, 2002. London
Wise, Michael, Abegg, Martin, Cook, Edward, *The Dead Sea Scrolls,* Harper Collins, 1999. London
Woods, George, Henry, *Herodotus Book II,* Rivingtons, London, 1897
Woolley, Benjamin, *The Queens's Conjuror,* Harper Collins, 2001. London
Wylie, Rev. J. A., *History of the Scottish Nation, Volume 1,* 1886, publisher unknown
Dr G.K Zollschan, Dr J.F Schumaker and Dr G.F. Walsh, *Exploring the Paranormal,* Prism Unity, 1989. London

Other Sources

Dictionary of Beliefs and Religions, Wordsworth. 1995.
Dictionary of Phrase and Fable, Wordsworth. 1995.
Dictionary of Science and Technology, Wordsworth Edition. 1995.
Dictionary of the Bible, Collins. 1974.
Dictionary of the Occult, Geddes and Grosset. 1997.
Dictionary of World Folklore, Larousse. 1995

Index

Action Comics 97
Alchemy and religion **Ch2**,52
Ancient Wisdom .... v, viii, xi, xiv, 10,11,23,54,55,65,74,109,**117**,137
animal magnetism, healing and hypnotism 133,134
Archidoxa Medicinae 5
Aristotle 5
Avicenna 5,7,8
Azoth 3,4
Balfour, Arthur. M.P. and Prime Minister. 111,116
Bat, etymology 85,100
Bell, Joseph 115
Bilderberg 31
Cabala 6,25,28,120
Caduceus 3
Cagliostro **23**,24-30,34,111,145
Canute, King 137-139
Captain Nemo 48
Cathars vi
Ciardi, John 135
Clement of Alexandria 126
Conan Doyle, Sir Arthur ix,73,77,82,91,**Ch7**,102,*103*,104–118,121
Conan Doyle and ancient wisdoms 109
Conan Doyle and freemasonry 107–109,111,117
Conan Doyle and the *Nuctemeron* 109–110
Conan Doyle, and the Jesuits 102,103,117,118
Conan Doyle, Kingsley (Sir Arthur's son) 112
Constantinople 2
Crowborough, home of Rosicrucianism 105
Crowley, Aleister 91,115,121, *122*
Crystalline structures 126,**127**,128–133
Dark Matter 125,126,130,136
Datura - use in Egyptian theurgy 122
Dee, Dr John 23
Doyle, Richard - artist and designer 112
Draco 80
Dracula 39,71,*72*,75,77,**78**,*79*–87,89,90,97,100,121
Drugs in Egyptian spiritual and magical life. 122
Druids and the sacred serpent 83
Eastern Order *81*
Emoto, Dr Masaru - water crystal photography 128,134
ESP, and Conan Doyle 104
Finger, Bill 92,97,99,101
Freemasons .... v,vi,xxi,23,*24*,27–29,31,43,51–55,59–62,65,67,69,74–78, ... 82,84,89,90,107–9,111,117,122,146
Freud, Siegmund - Psychoanalyst 93
Galen 4,5,7,8
Gardner, Edward - theosophist 112
Gnostics vi,xv–xvi,2,8,11,15,51,52,56,58,60,61,88,109,114,124,132,146
Golden Eye/Geometry 10
Gothic revival 73

Gothic style **72**,73,76–78,84,89,90
Grandmaster of the Knights of St John 20
Gustav Bord 5
Hakim, Caliph of the Fatimite 15
Hartmann, Dr Franz, theosophist 3
Helmont (Jan Baptista Van Helmont) 4,120
Henbane - use in Egyptian theurgy 122
Hermetic philosophy 2,6,8,29,58,105
Hesse, Hermann - on Nature xiv
Hetzel, Pierre-Jules 53,54,66,67,69
Hippocrates 4
Hitler, Adolf 10,37,146
Houdini, Harry *110*,111
Hoyle, Sir Fred, Astronomer 124
Hugo, Victor 51,53,66,67,74
Huxley, Aldous 35,44
Huxley, Julian 44,45
Irving, Sir Henry 76,77,89,90
Jac Carpus of Bologne,early doctor 4
Jacob's ladder and Quartz crystal 131
James Gardner - complexity theorist 134
Jesuits 22,103
Kane, Bob **92**,93–101,105
Knights of Malta - see Knights of St John
Knights of St John, ... 3,14,15,17–23,24,26,28–31,33,71
Knights of St John, and Blackwater 32
Knights Templar vi,17,18,31,48,143,146,147
Knut - see Canute, King
La Franc-Maconnerie en France 5
La Messe Noire (The Black Mass) J.Bricaud 120
Lamy, Michel 74,145
Le Fanu, Sheridan 78
lenin and trotsky 46
Levi, Eliphas; freemason. 27,52,104,105,108–111,120,145
Light spectrum and the crystal 124,135
Lillith, serpent deity 89
Luther, Martin 1,7
Madam Blavatsky, ... v,7,82,87,105,114,143
Mandalas 132
Manuel Pinto da Fonseca. **20**,21–29,30,34
Martinist Order 119,120
Mercury, use in medicine 4
Mesmer, Franz Anton and mesmerism 133,134
Mustapha Pasha 21
Natural Ratio xiv,xx,10,39
Nautilus 48,63,65
Newton, Sir Isaac 135
Opium – use in Egyptian theurgy 122
Oporinus of Basel University 3,5
Papus – See Encausse, Dr Gerard 119
Paracelsus and Italian Army 4
Philosopher's Stone 3,28
Paracelsus, doctor and alchemist **Ch1**,*1,6,*1–11,34,52,59,64,71,100,132
Paragranum 7

Pineal gland 133-4
Planck, Max - on 'The Matrix' 126-7
Poe, Edgar Allen 51,52,56,74,102,103,109
Price, Harry Founder of the National Laboratory for Psychical Research 121
Professor Moriarty 105,115-6
Quantum entanglement and ESP 132
Quantum information channel 133
Quantum Physics 132
Robin/Dick Grason 98
Sand, George 53
Seal of Solomon 8
Serotonin - effect on well being 133
Serpent/snake as symbol 3,26,27,28,29,80,83-91,92,100,101,113,143
Sgt Pepper's Lonely Hearts Club Album 121
Sherlock Holmes 102-5,107,109,111,112-7
Society of Psychical Research 105,107,111,117,121
Spiritualism 108,111,112,115,118
St Augustine 126
St Germain, Comte de 29,34
Steinbeck, John 124
Stoker, Bram 29,39,**Ch5**,71-91,92,100,110,114,120,121
Temples - as a symbol of universe and nature xvi
The Batman/Bruce Wayne 92,93,94,98,99,101
The Great Khan 3
The Illuminati 37,103,105
The King's chamber, Gt Pyramid 130
The Lair of the White Worm 77,87,88,89
The Log from the Sea of Cortez 124
The Rosicrucians 23,51,52,54,60-65,69,74,77,105,120,145
The Sign of the White Horse 1,3,5,7,9,11
Theosophists 3,7,74,77,83,86,87,108,112
Vampire, etymology 84
Vampires 30,72,75,78,79,81,83,85,96,99,**100**
van Helmont 4,120
van Helsing 79,86,87
Verne, Jules xii,43,**48**,49-52,54-58,60,61,63,65,67-70,71,73,89,100,102,145
Vlad lll, The Impaler 80
Weishaupt, Adam 29,103
Wells, H. G. viii,xii,7,**Ch3**,34-47,48,53,71,83,105,121,146
Wells, H. G. and freemasonry 43,
Wells, H. G. - *A Modern Utopia* 36,37,41
Wells, Hitler and the World State 37,146
Wells, H. G. *War of the Worlds* 38,39
Welles, Orson 38
Wendell Holmes, Oliver 115
Winston Churchill 10,44,105
Zorro, ...95

Other titles available from The Temple Publications

Royston Cave - Used by Saints or Sinners, **Sylvia Beamon**
ISBN 978-0-9557400-0-8
£ 16.99

Royston Cave-Used by Saints or Sinners? puts Royston's unique cave, so remarkably engraved with religious figures, pagan and Masonic symbols, into its historical context. It explores similarities between carvings and graffiti found in Hertfordshire, Cambridgeshire and elsewhere in Britain and Europe.

This fascinating book explains the historical influences of the Order of the Knights Templar and their rival crusading order, The Knights Hospitallers, who later inherited most their estates. It shows how the cave's structure bears comparison with the Church of The Holy Sepulchre in Jerusalem, which was at the heart of the Templar's world.

Its original research provides a wealth of information on:

The formation of the Templars
The history and enigma of Royston cave
Their commercial enterprises and banking system
Their cult and esoteric knowledge and their eventual downfall
Mediaeval carvings and symbols

This book will be relevant for Historians, Archaeologists or those wishing to explore the cave and the many other exciting historic and Templar sites throughout Europe.

The God Kings of England, **Hugh Montgomery**
ISBN 978-0-9555970-4-6
£ 11.99

Following on from *The God-Kings of Europe, The God-Kings of England,* continues the Saga of the great Ulvungar Dynasty. It shows that there was a plan to counter the hegemony of Roman Christianity, by counter attacking, first with Viking raids and later by conquest and settlement. This is the tale of the Ulvungars and their attempt to conquer England, under the leadership of Danish Kings such as Sweyn Forkbeard and Canute. They were opposed by their Odonic Anglo-Saxon cousins such as Alfred and Aethelred. The Ulvungars would take control by force of arms. One branch would take England; another would take control of Normandy. Ultimately, they would combine after the Battle of Hastings in the Anglo-Norman Dynasty that would found the Angevin Empire.

This book shows the web of marriages and alliances and the detailed planning that went into the final push that culminated at the Battle of Hastings. It shows how the Davidic line of Jesus was protected by the Odonic Kings of England and Dukes of Normandy.

In the appendices the author traces and explains who William the Conqueror's real ancestors were and shows detailed genealogies.

The Star Temple of Avalon, **Nicholas Mann & Philippa Glasson**

ISBN 978-0-9555970-8-4

£ 11.99

Countless myths and legends attest to the ancient sanctity of the Isle of Avalon. Yet archaeologists have long been puzzled by the absence of material evidence for prehistoric activity upon the hills of Glastonbury. This book provides decisive proof of the island's especial importance to our distant ancestors, by showing how its unique conjunction of landscape with key celestial movements would have indicated its extraordinary sanctity to Neolithic peoples, even to their Mesolithic forebears. Because of the intimate relationship between its holy hills and the pathways of sun, moon and stars, Avalon would have been understood as an exceptionally potent spiritual sanctuary, a place of otherworldly power.

Nicholas Mann and Philippa Glasson reveal the site of an ancient astronomical observatory at the heart of the Avalonian landscape. They show how prehistoric sky-watchers appear to have modelled key parts of the island, including the Tor and the summit of St Edmund's Hill, to refine their celestial observations. The Isle of Avalon was truly an ancient "temple of the stars".

Gwyn **-Ancient god of Glastonbury and key to the Glastonbury Zodiac, Yuri Leitch**

ISBN 978-0-9555970-1-5

£ 11.99

GWYN - Ancient god of Glastonbury and key to the Glastonbury Zodiac, is the debut book written and illustrated by Glastonbury based artist and researcher, Yuri Leitch. Adorned with many of his own beautiful illustrations, and quotes from arcane medieval Welsh manuscripts, the author hopes that this book will educate, uplift and inspire the reader's imagination.

'Gwyn' is the culmination of six years of contemplation, historical research and investigation into the sacred landscape of Somerset's unique landmark, Glastonbury Tor.

To the ancient Britons, this isle in the marshes, later named 'Glastonbury' by the Saxons, was known as Ynys Witrin or (The Glass Isle). This was their beloved sacred ground, the threshold of 'Annwn' - (their 'Otherworld' paradise.) Gwyn was the protective warrior god of 'Ynys Witrin' and the British 'Lord of Paradise'.

The book takes the reader back to the beginning of the 1st century - to the tribal society of the Native Britons specific to this area; the tribe that are known to us as the Durotriges. We glimpse their spiritual world by looking at The Children of Don; the Durotriges' pantheon of gods, goddesses and specifically Gwyn ap Nudd, the ancient god of Glastonbury. By doing this, we begin to understand Ynys Witrin as their most sacred ground

The author deals with the Roman invasion of Britain, and of how these ancient Britons adapted to their new Romano-British lifestyle. Despite their cultural changes the Durotriges continued to use Ynys Witrin as their sacred island at least up until the 5th century.

Controversially, this view challenges the popular legend that Jesus' kinsman, Joseph of Arimathea, founded a Christian church at Glastonbury in the 1st century - Yuri explains that whist Christians were the enemies of Rome well into the 3rd century, and that the lack of any archaeological remains indicating Christian presence until the 5th century shows how Glastonbury probably functioned as a sacred burial ground until the Dark Ages.

Gwyn also accounts for the first Christian missionaries of the 5th century who made very deliberate attempts to banish the old god from Glastonbury Tor.

By taking the reader step by step through medieval Welsh literature, Yuri Leitch explains how Gwyn has an intimate link with many of Glastonbury's unusual characteristics. The Tor's, it's placement on the St. Michael Line alignment with the Mid Winter sun-roll up the Tor and most curiously, with the landscape enigma of the Glastonbury Zodiac.

This is the tale of the Saxon invasion of Britain and the mass exodus of the native Britons from their homeland and their sacred isle. It tells the evocative tale of Centwine, the Saxon king of Wessex, who 'pushed the Britons to the sea' in the 7th century and the forced retreat into Wales, Cornwall and Brittany and beyond.

Here is some of the history, giving rise to the legendary tales of 'Avalon' and the sacred 'Otherworld' and- related faerie-realm mythology. Gwyn, the Lord of Paradise, is diminished by time and the newly imported traditions to become the 'King of the Fairies'. And then finally debased into the 'Demon King' of the Celtic Hades by ignorance; in this book you will discover the true god of Glastonbury.

The Temple Publications
PO Box 47
Watchet
Somerset
TA23 0WT
United Kingdom
www.thetemplepublications.com